INTO JAP...

INTO JAPAN

A STARTER KIT FOR UNDERSTANDING
JAPANESE SOCIETY

TIM ODAGIRI

OWANI PRESS

Seattle • Tokyo

Publisher's Cataloging-in-Publication Data
    Names: Odagiri, Tim, author.
    Title: Into Japan : a starter kit for understanding Japanese society / Tim Odagiri.
    Series: Understand in One Afternoon
    Description: Seattle, WA; Tokyo, Japan: Owani Press, 2023.
    Identifiers: LCCN: 2023917257 | ISBN: 978-0-9964654-4-1 (paperback) | 978-0-9964654-5-8 (ebook)
    Subjects: LCSH Japan. | Political culture--Japan. | Japan--History. | Japan--Politics and government--1945-. | Japan--Economic conditions. | Japan--Social conditions--1945- | BISAC HISTORY / Asia / Japan | POLITICAL SCIENCE / Civics & Citizenship
    Classification: LCC JQ1681 .O33 2023 | DDC 342.52--dc23

ISBN-13: 978-0-9964654-4-1 (paperback)
ISBN-13: 978-0-9964654-5-8 (ebook)

CONTENTS

INTRODUCTION

I know what you are thinking. "A book on Japanese government and history. Ugh! What could be more boring than that?" Perhaps you are right. I mean, this is Japan we are talking about! As a foreign resident living in this archipelago at the eastern edge of the world, you have direct access to the food, the artistry, and the technology of one of the most historically fascinating, culturally rich, and gastronomically delicious nations on earth. There are castles to explore that were once home to authentic samurai warriors, endless varieties of sushi and ramen, and bullet trains that will whisk you off to some of the most scenic and meaningful experiences of your life. Who has time to read about constitutions?

Japan is certainly amazing, but it didn't get that way by accident. The Japanese spent millennia transforming their island home into what it is today. During those centuries, they experienced political upheavals, a sobering number of natural disasters, and a world war that devastated major cities. Despite such tragedies, the people flourished, and by their ingenuity and fortitude, Japan became one of the most important and respected countries in history.

Naturally, there were key individuals that helped guide Japan's path: the fifteenth century shogun Tokugawa Ieyasu; the modern educator and founder of Keio University Fukuzawa Yukichi; authors and poets such as the country's first great novelist, Murasaki Shikibu. And don't forget the emperors.

You will no doubt find such eminent *dramatis personae* in the annals of other nations. But what makes Japan different is the expectation that ordinary citizens have a duty to fulfill their societal roles for the benefit of the country. Hierarchical social structures and distinct class divisions refined over the centuries have helped instill these obligations into the mindset of the populace. But this communal understanding is even codified in the text of Japan's postwar Constitution, which insists that rights and freedoms "shall be maintained by the constant endeavor of the people."

What about the immigrants? For several centuries, during Japan's *sakoku* period, the only duty placed on foreigners was that they turn their boats around and take their religion and their foul alien ways back home. But now Japan is open to all comers, for both tourism and residency. Some of these arrivals commit to Japan for the long run. More than three million foreigners now live in Japan on some kind of official visa, around 2.5 percent of the population. At least a quarter of these have opted for permanent residency. Add to that those who have already made the transition to naturalized citizenship and you now have a significant and established base of expats who call Japan their home.

I am one of those foreign residents. My relocation to Japan came with the understanding that I would enjoy many of the rights afforded to native citizens. Not all the rights, of course. I can't vote in elections, and some government jobs are off limits to me. Plus, there are various procedures that require more paperwork on my part due solely to my immigrant status. But overall, I enjoy the same benefits that Japanese citizens have access to.

This is where we must return to that constitutional stipulation concerning "the constant endeavor of the people." As a foreigner living in Japan, I have been guaranteed a legal grant of so many civil rights. But in line with societal expectations placed on the citizenry, those rights are paired with certain duties as expressed through cultural traditions and constitutional pronouncements.

Japan has a surprisingly high expectation for civic engagement, even down to mundane tasks like sorting garbage. These standards also apply to the knowledge of societal structures and cultural principles. Without a basic understanding of Japanese history and civic organization, it may be difficult or even impossible to perform some of the duties of residency that the native population does without even thinking about it.

This is why *Into Japan* exists, to provide tools that foreign residents need to better participate in Japanese society. A common frame of reference is essential for a functioning democracy. Some commentators link America's current woes with a reduction in shared experiences and diminished cultural literacy among its residents. As the number of immigrants in Japan grows, it is essential that these newcomers acquire a grounding in basic cultural expectations and civic responsibilities already common to everyone else. Without such training, misunderstandings and turmoil are inevitable.

This book provides a starting point for further cultural exploration. This short work will not make you an expert on Japanese society. Instead, the goal is to construct a core foundation on which newcomers can further build. As I wrote each chapter, I asked myself, "What do average adults in Japan still recall about history and civics from their high school social studies classes?" My hope is that by reading this and similar texts, foreign residents will be able to wander around Japan with some of those same foundational memories rattling around in their heads.

Some say that because Japan is a highly structured society with designated insiders and outsiders, there is no point in trying to fit in. But that is precisely why basic training in cultural literacy is necessary. Despite what the naysayers claim, it is possible to adapt to Japanese society. It might take many years to accomplish, perhaps even a generation or two, and anyone who is fresh off the boat will always feel ill-at-ease. But as we advance in our understanding of our new homeland, we will be ready to play the role that, frankly, the native population is already expecting us to perform.

Acknowledgments

If you ever decide to write your own book about Japan, I highly recommend a visit to the National Diet Library, Japan's equivalent to the Library of Congress in the United States. This government institution is stuffed with primary and secondary sources about Japan, its people, and its history. I was fortunate enough to spend several days on site engaged in research for this volume and had a chance to view key documents and memoranda covering the development of Japan's modern Constitution. Especially moving was *The Origin and Development of the Draft Constitution of Japan*, by Satō Tatsuo, one of the Japanese government officials who spearheaded the development of the document. An English edition is available if you want to read a first-hand account of history in the making.

I am also fortunate to have several people in my life who are skilled enough and blunt enough to review this book and offer essential corrections and insights. Since I know all their last names, I decided to mention them here in that order.

Harold Archer, a long-term Tokyo resident and infamous "car guy," provided big-picture insights, especially when he wisely told me to ditch the book's original bland title. He has also been a regular source of inspiration and guidance for Nihon Plus You (日本＋YOU), a new research center we are setting up to help foreign residents in Japan and the native Japanese population work together for their mutual benefit. (Stop by nihonplusyou.org if you are curious.)

Jon Heese provided feedback on the government and economics portions of this book, expertise he gained from being one of Japan's few foreign-born politicians. Although he was busy serving the citizens of Tsukuba Science City and Ibaraki Prefecture as their elected representative, he still found time to offer valuable observations on the text and on the political process in Japan.

Ishikawa Kaoru, an *éminence grise* of Japanese foreign diplomacy, also read through the book's government-related content. As a former Japanese ambassador to both Egypt and Canada, his knowledge of the Japanese governmental systems is nothing to be sneezed at, and it was my honor to have him scan through the text and offer key improvements.

Dermot Vibert's understanding of Japanese history, especially in a global context, is amazing. This isn't surprising given that he himself came to Japan decades ago from elsewhere on the globe and now spends his days dealing with international business concerns. I'm blessed that he could use his knowledge to improve several of this book's chapters.

Brandon Whittaker was my first choice to look through the book's coverage of the Japanese Constitution. He was once the Executive Editor of the *Harvard Business Law Review*, but now resides here in Japan and works as a professor of law. He provided corrective feedback on the government portions and kept me on my toes with grammar.

As always, my wife Maki and son Spencer restrained themselves from rolling their eyes each time I mentioned the book. Instead, they offered support and encouragement in spades. Love you both!

Japanese Names

Before jumping into the text, a quick word about names: This book adopts the Japanese pattern for names of Japanese origin, placing the surname first followed by the given name. For emperors, the regnal name is typically used rather than the pre-ascent given name. That is, the reigning monarch in the mid-twentieth century is listed as Emperor Shōwa, not Hirohito. Exceptions are made for timeline or stylistic purposes.

CHAPTER ONE

Japanese History

Studying history is hard, mostly because it keeps distracting you with side tangents. Back in high school, when I was learning about the American Revolutionary War, our teacher constantly mentioned the situation in England and Continental Europe. That stuff was happening an ocean away, yet because history never occurs in a vacuum, it all mattered.

When it comes to Japan, though, things will be as vacuum-packed as you are likely to find. As an island nation, it was partially protected—sometimes for centuries—from bothersome external influences. Not completely, mind you. Sometimes the Mongols or the Dutch would show up. But then a divine wind or an imperial edict would make them all go away, allowing Japanese history to continue unabated.

Despite this pattern of isolation, the wider world still managed to imprint itself on Japan's culture and institutions. The influence from China is incalculable, first from its Confucian worldview and jurisprudence and later from its written language. The Europeans arrived centuries later, bringing their guns and their God. Then the Americans showed up in the mid-1800s, followed by the rest of the planet during World War II. These interactions with the outside world were often dramatic, but for the purposes of our quick read through history, they were brief and distinct.

A second aspect of Japanese history that makes it easier to study is its unbroken imperial line. The oldest continuous dynasty on earth, the current emperor's lineage stretches back—at least by tradition—to several centuries before the time of Christ. This fixed national thread lets us trace key events along a persistent path that, though often messy, is eminently definitional. Be sure to grab on tightly to that lineage, as we are going to move with bullet-train speed through Japan's timeline.

Japan's First Residents

The initial residents of the Japanese archipelago arrived in multiple waves from the Asian mainland. Known collectively as the Jōmon peoples, the first settlers came over on foot, thanks to a land bridge that connected northern Hokkaidō to the continent 30,000 years ago.

When people mention the Jōmon today, they typically refer to the large-scale migration to northern and central Japan that began around 14,000 years ago, a few thousand years before the land bridge dissipated. These hunter-gatherers lived a stone-age existence, relying on fishing and hunting for their sustenance, although they later added some basic agriculture. They are remembered and named for their clay pots decorated with cord patterns.

A separate group of mainlanders, the Ainu, crossed over that same land bridge by way of Okhotsk and Kamchatka, the northeast extremes of modern-day Russia. While anthropologically classified as Jōmon, this second group possessed a distinct language and culture, one that was able to endure the arrival of the native Japanese. Thousands of Ainu still reside in Japan today, primarily in Hokkaidō and Tōhoku.

Unlike those indigenous Ainu, the Jōmon proper died out by 300 BC, although some mingled into the newly arrived Yayoi population, the true ancestors of modern Japanese. Without land access, this new human wave came by ocean waves, landing on the western Japanese coast from the Korean peninsula starting around 1000 BC. Instead of bone-tipped bows and arrows, the Yayoi understood metalworking and rice-cultivation methods, allowing them to quickly supplant the less developed Jōmon as they moved northward. In addition to their own distinct style of pottery, the early Yayoi employed bronze and iron tools, and possessed a more structured social hierarchy than the earlier inhabitants. By the mid-third century AD, when historians mark the end of that period, upwards of four million Yayoi lived across the main body of Japan.

Japan's Legendary Founding

I know you are itching to find out what happened to these Japanese progenitors. But before you start scratching, we need to jump back nearly a thousand years to the officially documented founding of the Japanese nation, and to the celestial events that led to that majestic start. As our reference, we will use the *Kojiki*, the "Account of Ancient Matters." Empress Genmei (707-715) commissioned its three volumes of classical Chinese text in AD 711, seeking an apologia for the authority and lineage of the ruling Yamato clan. And boy did she get it. The second and third volumes contain typical biographical fare, a review of Japan's initial thirty-three emperors, only a small portion of which is considered factual or exciting. The good stuff appears in the first scroll, where you discover the nation's supernatural foundations, the official eighth-century statement on the divine origins of the imperial line.

In the beginning were the *kami*, the gods of Japan's traditional Shinto religion. Originally just three in number, they begot themselves into a large community, regularly engaging in the kind of ancient deity exploits that westerners have come to expect from the Greek and Roman pantheons.

Of particular importance to the imperial line was Amaterasu Ōmikami, the demigod associated with sun and sky. The brightness of her countenance was literally like the sun, and a shroud of darkness momentarily enveloped the world when she hid in a cave after a spat with her brother Susanoo. Failing to get her own son to take the job, Amaterasu put her grandson Ninigi in charge of earthly lands. In a not-that-surprising twist, he and his descendants—Japan's emperors—were cursed to live as mortals after he bungled a marriage engagement.

One of Ninigi's grandchildren—and therefore, the great-great-grandchild of the sun goddess—became Japan's first ruler, Emperor Jimmu. He ascended the throne on February 11, 660 BC, the first day of spring in the lunar calendar and one of the most auspicious days for Chinese zodiac fans. (Some scholars believe that a few of the emperors listed in the *Kojiki* were fabricated to pad the timeline back to this date.) As symbols of Jimmu's authority, Ninigi bequeathed him the three Imperial Regalia of Japan: a sword, a bronze mirror, and a precious jewel once belonging to Amaterasu herself. Three sacred items matching those descriptions are still passed from one emperor to the next, although given their hallowed status, the current monarch has never gazed upon them directly.

A second key work, the *Nihon Shoki* ("Chronicle of Japan"), appeared a decade after the *Kojiki*. It covers some of the same material justifying Japan's divine right of kings and adds details on the next eight emperors. Scholars who care about things like accuracy view coverage of the final three emperors positively but are more critical of the historical details that preceded them. Some may scoff at the fanciful tales documented in the *Kojiki* and the *Nihon Shoki*. But even if you ignore absolutely everything before Emperor Number Thirty-Eight (Tenji, 668-671), Japan still ends up having the longest, continuous monarchy on earth. This feels borderline supernatural given all that happened in Japan across the centuries. Speaking of which, let's find out what's up with those Yayoi.

The Yamato Period and the Rise of National Governance

The Yayoi were spread out across Japan, but that doesn't mean they were in sync. Known as the land of Wa by Chinese officials of that era, the Japan of AD 250 housed around a hundred identifiable states. One in particular drew the attention of contemporaneous Chinese historians, a domain called Yamatai, ruled by Queen Himiko. Tracking down the actual location has proved difficult, but it is often linked to Yamato, a state located near present-day Nara that served as the nexus for Japanese nobility over the next five and a half centuries.

The Yamato Period is divided into two parts of roughly the same length. The first is the Kofun Period, running up through 538. "Kofun" refers to the thousands of keyhole-shaped burial mounds so popular with deceased local and national leaders of that era. But before they were buried, these regional managers, aristocrats, and area rulers were busy strengthening relations between states across Japan. Through strategic marriages, diplomatic arrangements, and the occasional battle, this federation of independent states extended from the southern border of Tōhoku clear down to Kyūshū, even seeping into a portion of the Korean peninsula.

Those associations transitioned into a unified rule during the early sixth century under Emperor Keitai, who as head of the Yamato tribe decided to make his oversight national. He and his issue ruled the country from the seat of government in Asuka, south of Nara, and the Asuka Period (538-710) is named after this powerful capital.

As Yamato influence spread, so did the newly arrived Buddhist religion, thanks in part to the parallel introduction of a comprehensive writing system from China, both of which were adjusted to Japanese tastes. The minting of coins also dates from this period, an indication of the economic growth and importance of the era, especially in trade relations with kingdoms in China and Korea.

The Yamato Court was able to exert control over its vast domain thanks to intricate bureaucratic systems at local, regional, and national levels. Some clans, including the powerful Soga family, became managerial specialists, enabling their influence to intermingle with that of the aristocrats. This framework of government control supported by complex, hierarchical rules and a defined bureaucratic class has remained the norm in Japan across the centuries, up to the present day.

The Taika Reforms and the Shift to Nara

Beyond their managerial prowess, the Soga clan were also adept with the sword, cementing their hold on power by trouncing the rival Mononobe tribe at the Battle of Shigisan in 587. The *Nihon Shoki* gives particular accolades to Prince Shōtoku of the Soga line, and let me count the ways he was awesome beyond the battlefield: son of Emperor Yōmei; imperial regent for three decades during the reign of his aunt, Empress Suiko; author of a new and improved Japanese Constitution; reformer of the court system, replacing seniority with meritocracy; founder of the Japanese strain of Buddhism and author of key commentaries; builder of temples; writer of the first Japanese-language book; coiner of Japan as "Land of the Rising Sun." Need I say more about this overachiever?

Prince Shōtoku died in 622 while still in his forties, and with him passed his vision for national governance based on social harmony. Instead, confusion erupted within the court. The rival Nakatomi clan chose this moment to oust the Soga and dominate the imperial line, ushering in a time of Great Changes (*"taika"*), quite literally through the "Taika Reforms" of 645.

Prince Naka no Ōe and Nakatomi clan leader Kamatari set up their new imperial capital in Nara, strengthening and centralizing national authority under the emperor, aided by loyal aristocrats and bureaucrats. The Nakatomi were indispensable in this task, prompting Emperor Tenji in 668 to bestow on the family the title of "Fujiwara," the name by which they are typically referred to today. The court also developed an official history of the imperial line—the aforementioned *Kojiki* and *Nihon Shoki*—to justify the new status quo.

A New Capital in Kyōto

Despite the great changes of the Taika era, the court opted to retain and expand on Shōtoku's Buddhist vision for the nation, spreading its religious norms and worldview beyond the capital and out to subordinate states across the archipelago. As good as this sounds, separation of church and state wasn't a thing yet, and by the mid-eighth century, the court and clergy were vying for power. Rather than battle priest after priest, Emperor Kammu instead picked up the entire capital and moved it to Kyōto in 781, leaving the Nara Period and the Buddhist holy men behind. This translocation marked the start of the Heian Period, an era of imperial fragmentation that stretched out over four centuries.

The breakdown didn't happen right away. The emperor had a shiny new palace minus the clerical intrigue. The Fujiwara solidified their power further by marrying into the imperial family. Emperor Kammu even managed to quell the bothersome Tōhoku Ainu tribes by appointing Japan's first military shogun, a victory that eventually brought all Honshū island under imperial authority.

Perhaps you detected the flaw already: Letting a power-hungry family insert itself into the ruling line. By 850, Kammu's offspring were powerless to stop the…well, let's simply say they were powerless. The Fujiwara used their familial rights and administrative prowess to dictate who would ascend the throne, giving them complete control over the court system and its ruler. But their hegemony had geographic and institutional limits. Anti-Fujiwara aristocrats, many of whom wielded regional authority far from Kyōto, made cunning use of the bureaucracy to shift managerial, land-control, and tax-collecting authority away from the court.

Fujiwara dominance lasted a mere two centuries, ending abruptly when rival courtiers lifted Go-Sanjō to the throne in 1068. He immediately cleared out key Fujiwara leaders and restructured the tax system to ensure greater management over national matters from Kyōto, under the direct authority of the throne.

Go-Sanjō's rule was effective but short, lasting just five years until his death. His offspring managed to keep the Fujiwara at bay, but all that political infighting couldn't have been pleasant. By 1086, emperors had devised a system of "cloistered rule" where the new emperor would quickly abdicate after appointing a successor. The retiree would move to a nearby monastery for meditation and aesthetic edification, euphemisms for "controlling everything from behind the scenes." Through this split-leadership system, the throne managed to temper both Fujiwara agitators and the rising military class through the end of the twelfth century.

We know this in part through court histories and other documents, typically written in formal, government-friendly Chinese. But the Heian era also saw the rise of literary contributions, primarily from court women. These were penned using standardized phonetic *hiragana* and *katakana* syllabaries that allowed for the full range of Japanese communication. The most famous of these works is Murasaki Shikibu's *The Tale of Genji*, an epic romance that, though fictionalized, communicates historically useful details about court life under Fujiwara rule. Completed around 1020, it is considered by many to be the world's first novel.

Samurai Clans Battle their Way to Power

Inviting the Fujiwara into the imperial family wasn't the only *faux pas* from the early Heian period. Emperor Kammu's decision to appoint all-powerful military leaders—the shogun—to deal with border skirmishes also worked to destabilize the throne.

With each military victory, the court heaped rewards on top commanders, often in the form of land-cultivation rights called *shiki*, making these generals vassals of the state, and financially secure ones to boot. Local clan leaders, grateful for the protection, did the paperwork for these transactions. The warrior chiefs, grateful in turn for being upgraded to landed gentry, began directing their loyalty toward the clans. These soldiers were so, so far from the capital, and they also had all the swords and abundant land, so, why not? As their holdings grew, the generals were able to offer rewards to their own subordinate soldiers and family members, building loyal armies that no longer had to rely on the court or local *shōen* administrators for their daily rice. By the mid-twelfth century, these samurai corps were powerful enough to challenge the Heian government, both regionally and in the capital.

Kyōto was slow to notice the danger. The year was 1155, and a sixteen-year-old Emperor Konoe sat on the throne while his father (former Emperor Toba) and older brother (former Emperor Sutoku) pulled strings and levers from their cloistered retreats. Konoe died suddenly, prompting Toba to appoint another of his sons as Emperor Go-Shirakawa instead of letting Sutoku decide. When Toba died the following year, Sutoku decided to act, which triggered competing Fujiwara regent factions to get involved— remember them?—who in turn called on the Minamoto and Taira samurai clans to literally battle it out for succession.

Go-Shirakawa's allies won that round (the Hōgen Rebellion), though they had to do it all over again during another mini civil war three years later (the Heiji Rebellion). Sure, the sitting emperor remained on the throne after each action. But the real victory took place within the samurai families, especially the Taira, the victors of the Heiji insurrection over the now-weakened Minamoto. Taira Kiyomori and other members of his family replaced key Fujiwara government figures, setting up a proto-shogunate under the successors of the abdicated and cloistered Emperor Go-Shirakawa.

Two decades later, the Minamoto rebounded from their earlier defeat and attacked their Taira rivals at the Battle of Uji, sparking a five-year national civil war that raged over land and sea. When the Gempei War culminated in 1185, the Minamoto had thoroughly trounced the Taira clan and the Heian court. Patriarch Minamoto Yoritomo declared himself shogun in 1192, setting up the new *bakufu* (military government) in distant Kamakura. The emperor still reigned in Kyōto with his court, carrying out the necessary administrative functions of government. But make no mistake: the samurai were in charge.

Military Governance in the Kamakura Period

To better control the palace, the new shogunate enlisted the Hōjō family as regents for the emperor. Like the Fujiwara before them, the Hōjō carefully directed imperial succession, ensuring that only shogun-friendly leaders acceded to the throne. There were bumps along the way, especially when Emperor Go-Toba attempted to overthrow his Hōjō keepers in the Jōkyū War of 1221; he failed. The infamous Mongol warlord Kublai Khan tried to invade Japan decades later, making two separate attempts in 1274 and 1281. Each time, a powerful *kamikaze* (divine wind) typhoon decimated the armada.

Although the bakufu kept winning, the financial outlays for those battles took their toll on the shogunate. The Hōjō also struggled, unable to resist the temptations of cushy palace life. By 1331, the sitting emperor, Go-Daigo, garnered sufficient fortitude and influence to seek restoration of the throne's authority. His first attempt that year fell short, earning him nothing more than exile to the Oki Islands, a good fifty-plus kilometers off Japan's western coast.

Just two years later, in 1333, Go-Daigo escaped his banishment and quickly assembled an army. Commander Nitta Yoshisada led troops loyal to the emperor against Kamakura that July, and when the fortress fell days later, the Hōjō leaders revealed their expectations for recovering power by committing suicide *en masse*.

Go-Daigo returned to Kyōto and immediately began the work of reestablishing imperial authority, the so-called Kenmu Restoration. Unfortunately for the emperor, a known traitor foiled his plans. Ashikaga Takauji, a former

Hōjō military commander, had switched sides after Go-Daigo's escape from Oki and was instrumental in assuring Kamakura's defeat. Ever the turncoat, Ashikaga conspired against Go-Daigo to capture the throne and become the shogun, splitting the seat of power into northern and southern courts—a time known as *nanboku-chō*—and triggering centuries of constant warfare.

Open Warfare During the Muromachi Period

In the northern Kyōto palace, Ashikaga selected Kōgon, the son of a former emperor, to become the first of six "pretender" monarchs. What was Go-Daigo to do but set up his own palace in exile, to the south in Yoshino, near Nara. The two courts battled for supremacy over the next six decades, and while the northern court was ostensibly ruling the country thanks to having a shogun in residence, the regional daimyo lords were left increasingly to govern their territories with little support from any sitting emperor.

By 1392, three more emperors had ruled from Yoshino, but as sometimes happens in these civil wars, the North prevailed over the South. That October, Go-Kameyama formally abdicated his claim, handing the Imperial Regalia over to Go-Komatsu, the sitting emperor in Kyōto. In theory, the two lines were to alternate reigns in a throne-sharing pact, but of course that never happened. And so, the southern line ended with Japan's ninety-ninth monarch, though there are individuals even today who do not accept those northern royal pretenders. Just after World War II, a descendant of Go-Kameyama demanded that Emperor Shōwa abdicate so that he could accede to the throne as the legitimate monarch. Neither Hirohito nor General MacArthur was convinced.

The northern court prevailed in large part because the Muromachi shogunate had the military might to enforce the claim. But Ashikaga authority was soon to go the way of Go-Daigo's line. After a rival clan assassinated shogun Ashikaga Yoshinori in 1441, the family's grip on power crumbled quickly. By 1464, they had run out of heirs, prompting then-shogun Ashikaga Yoshimasa to appoint his brother to succeed him. Then the unthinkable happened: Yoshimasa had a son, sparking a succession crisis.

Things escalated quickly, with the powerful Kyōto-area Hosokawa and Yamana clans lining up behind either the brother or the child, each seeking to take control of the bakufu. The bloodshed began in earnest in 1467, though by this time, the Ashikaga were so weak that they barely rose to the level of belligerent. Instead, the shogun immersed himself in cultural pursuits; while Yoshimasa fiddled with poetry and architecture, Kyōto burned.

Thus began the *Sengoku Jidai*, the rightly named "Warring States period." When its opening Ōnin War ended ten years later, the capital and any sense of national unity lay in ruins, though the fighting raged on. The Hosokawa took over the shogunate, but with the rival Ōuchi clan constantly trying to take control of the bakufu, numerous high-level assassinations, clan-on-clan warfare across the country, and peasant revolts becoming popular nationwide, there wasn't much left to oversee. During the 1550s, upstart subordinates betrayed and destroyed the Hosokawa and Ōuchi families, not that it brought any more stability. And in the midst of this mess, the Europeans showed up, starting with the Portuguese in 1543, literally adding gunpowder to the mix.

Renewed Unity in the Azuchi-Momoyama Period

Constant regional battles and treachery within clans provided abundant churn in local samurai leadership. Consider Owari Province, a district near present-day Nagoya that was fighting battles with bordering states and dealing with intra-clan rivalries. When clan chief Oda Nobuhide died suddenly in 1551, his sons, brothers, and pretty much anyone else with a hankering for military glory saw it as a chance to grasp authority. Oda Nobunaga, Nobuhide's oldest legitimate son and the father's hand-picked replacement, was just a teenager when the fights for succession broke out. It took seven years of death and destruction, but Nobunaga prevailed, uniting all Owari under his control.

He barely had time to clean his sword when Imagawa Yoshimoto, head of the eastern province of Suruga, decided to expand into Oda domains. Despite having only a few thousand soldiers, Nobunaga initiated a surprise counterattack while Imagawa's troops were still setting up for battle. The Owari killed Yoshimoto and defeated an invading army ten times their size, bringing ample glory to Nobunaga. He then turned west, and through a series of military victories and alliances, brought several provinces all the way to present-day Gifu under his authority.

By 1568, the disunity of the Sengoku Jidai was starting to get on Japan's nerves. Ashikaga Yoshiaki, brother of the recently betrayed and murdered shogun—which was surprisingly still an active title—approached Nobunaga in Gifu, imploring him to take over the capital and appoint Yoshiaki as the replacement shogun. Seeing this as his chance to unify the nation—and get the accolades—Nobunaga set his face toward Kyōto. He first had to get through intense resistance in Ōmi Province which, well, he did. Come November, Nobunaga was marching into Kyōto, dispersing the usurping Miyoshi puppet-masters, and installing Ashikaga Yoshiaki as the fifteenth (and final, for now) shogun. Oda's arrival at the capital marked the start of the Azuchi-Momoyama Period, the final phase of Japan's nationwide civil war.

Kyōto was okay, but Nobunaga still had a passion for an Oda-led unified Japan. The other samurai leaders found this plan wanting, but Nobunaga, being a ruthless military tyrant, went ahead anyway. Over the next fourteen years, he dominated Japan's central region, from Ōsaka and Kyōto in the west clear out beyond his Owari homeland in the east, before setting his sights on more remote provinces. The carnage was unspeakable; in one key campaign, Nobunaga's forces set fire to the monastic compound on Mount Hiei, killing thousands of monk-warriors and their families holed up inside.

After defeating anti-Nobunaga forces in 1573, Oda returned to Kyōto and exiled the shogun who, despite owing his position to Nobunaga, had joined in the battle against him. The emperor had no choice but to recognize Oda's authority, bringing an end to the Muromachi shogunate and cementing Nobunaga's reputation as the first Great Unifier of Japan.

Despite his merciless reputation, Oda established stable administrations in his wake, setting the stage for a later national peace. His exploits are too numerous to mention in this short history, but they would have been greater had he not been cut down in his forties. Akechi Mitsuhide, one of Oda's key generals, attempted to assassinate Nobunaga while the latter engaged in a tea ceremony at Honnō-ji temple in Kyōto on June 21, 1582. The reason for Mitsuhide's treachery is still unknown, but before he could complete the job, Nobunaga committed *seppuku* and his aide set fire to the temple so the body couldn't be captured. A few weeks later, Nobunaga's retainer Toyotomi Hideyoshi took revenge on Mitsuhide, who died fleeing the battle.

With Oda Nobunaga gone, Toyotomi took up his mantle as Japan's second Great Unifier, ultimately bringing order to the whole of western Japan by the end of the 1580s using less ruthless means than his predecessor. He then joined with former Nobunaga ally Tokugawa Ieyasu—head of the Matsudaira clan and destined to become the third Great Unifier—to quell the eastern domains. Together, they overcame the powerful Hōjō family, ruling the east coast Sagami district from their castle in Odawara. As spoils, Hideyoshi granted Ieyasu the Hōjō's former domains in the Kantō plain while reserving for himself the districts between Sagami and Kyōto.

The long, brutal era of warfare dissipated with the victory at Odawara Castle. As regent and chancellor of Japan, Toyotomi Hideyoshi returned to the capital and negotiated terms of peace with the remaining districts who had not yet submitted to imperial authority. But it wasn't all daisies and sunshine. Domestic rebellions cropped up here and there, and the nation also got embroiled in battles on the Korean peninsula. Then there was that time when the regent had twenty-six Christians tortured and crucified in Nagasaki. He also put members of his own family to death to ensure that his son would inherit the regency. But on the whole, his scheme for bringing Japan together was less brutal and geographically more extensive than the work done by Oda Nobunaga.

Peace at Last in the Edo Period

Hideyoshi's son Hideyori rose to regent on the passing of his father in 1598, but as he was just five years old, a team of five adults performed the actual regenting. But what acting regent in his right mind would defer to a toddler when the power of Japan was at his disposal? Well, not all the power. There was still the issue of Tokugawa Ieyasu over in Kantō, now the most powerful daimyo in the country. Ishida Mitsunari, one of the five, decided to eliminate the Tokugawa threat, and marched 80,000 troops eastward to present-day Gifu. The October 21, 1600, Battle of Sekigahara proved decisive, lifting Ieyasu above his Toyotomi attackers and bringing the Azuchi-Momoyama Period to an abrupt end. Over the next three years, Ieyasu continued to extend his authority over the nation, with the sitting emperor having no choice but to defer to the new all-powerful shogun.

Tokugawa Ieyasu announced his new shogunate on March 24, 1603, from Edo Castle, the present-day central Tōkyō home of Japan's imperial family. He ruled only a short time, abdicating just two years later and passing authority to his son Hidetada. The son in turn abdicated after eleven years, making Ieyasu's grandson Iemitsu the new shogun. Toyotomi Hideyori continued to be an irritant throughout these reigns, but that ended when Ieyasu laid siege to Hideyoshi's favorite son at Ōsaka Castle in 1615, destroying the Toyotomi family and removing the final obstacle to Edo supremacy.

Building on the work of the first two Great Unifiers, Ieyasu and his offspring established a stable national bakufu by instituting laws that gave a reasonable amount of authority to all players, but not too much. The new vassalage system allowed provinces to manage most aspects of their domains provided that they deferred to Edo on national matters. This included *sankin-kōtai*, a law requiring provincial leaders to alternate residency repeatedly between costly Edo and their own regional dwellings, reducing opportunities for well-financed rebellions. The emperor's court remained in place in Kyōto and powerful temples persisted, but these institutions were also expected to adhere to Tokugawa expectations.

Foreigners and Christians were a different matter. Japan had had enough of Spanish and Portuguese meddling in its affairs, especially after a 1637 quasi-Christian uprising in Kyūshū. The shogunate banished all Iberians and their Catholic beliefs, limiting continued European trade to the Dutch—who conveniently were also at war with Spain and Portugal—and then only through the island port of Dejima, off the coast of Nagasaki. This seclusion (*sakoku*) of the island nation applied to Asian traders as well, though licenses were granted to specific countries. The isolation prevented Japan from modernizing along European standards, but it also helped to protect the country from colonization and cross-cultural contamination as it healed from centuries of warfare. The samurai ranks, no longer useful for battle, became protectors of domestic affairs, allowing inter-province trade and cultural practices to flourish in an atmosphere of martial peace.

Edo had a good run, especially with living standards, literacy, security, and artistry expanding throughout the land for two and a half centuries. The division of labor between the shogun in Edo and the emperor in Kyōto was clear and stable, and the shogunate even managed to bring the wayward northern island of Hokkaidō under its purview.

Then the western powers returned. On July 14, 1853, American Commodore Matthew Perry steamed into Edo Bay with ten "black ships" (*kuro fune*) and a letter from President Millard Fillmore, asking politely but firmly that Japan establish diplomatic and trade relations with the New World. Japan signed its first treaty of friendship with the United States the following spring, adding similar relations with the European powers soon after.

Despite its cultural depth, Japan was no match militarily for these new arrivals, and one look at the trade agreements it felt compelled to sign made that disparity clear. Ii Naosuke, the Tokugawa shogunate's chief minister, had signed the initial trade agreement with the United States in 1858, in direct defiance of Emperor Kōmei's objections. Regional daimyos, including those from the powerful Satsuma Province in Kyūshū and Mito Province in central Honshū, viewed the lopsided treaties as a national embarrassment. In retribution for this shame, *rōnin* samurai assassinated Minster Ii in March 1860, at the Sakurada Gate, just a stone's throw away from Edo Castle. This Sakuradamon Incident kicked off years of violence that pitted the shogunate against provincial samurai who objected to Edo's dominance in both domestic and international matters.

The Meiji Restoration and the New Empire of Japan

Satsuma, Chōshū, Tosa, and other provinces were tired of Edo pulling every imperial string. They lined up behind Prince Mutsuhito, who at age fourteen acceded to the throne as the Emperor Meiji on February 3, 1867. With the combined influence of the Chrysanthemum Throne and the western provinces—not to mention their samurai armies—Edo blinked, triggering the last shogun, Tokugawa Yoshinobu, to resign in November that same year.

The pro-monarchy provinces acted immediately. While Satsuma samurai commander Saigō Takamori waited outside the palace with his own troops and those from Chōshū, Satsuma leader Ōkubo Toshimichi and co-conspirators from other powerful provinces and the court called for a return to absolute imperial rule on January 3, 1868. In the face of this Meiji Restoration, the retired shogun Yoshinobu and the like-minded northern provinces had a change of heart, raising an army of 15,000 and, with their French allies, confronted the emperor's forces.

The ensuing Boshin War threatened to pull Japan back into a warring-states mindset, but Takamori and his modernized forces defended Kyōto and began pursuing the Tokugawa belligerents. Yoshinobu surrendered in Edo that June, but his loyal troops continued to defend their shogun, eventually crossing the Tsugaru Strait into Hokkaidō, and declaring a new Republic of Ezo. Imperial forces defeated these holdouts in June 1869, eliminating the last vestiges of the defunct Tokugawa shogunate.

Under Meiji guidance, Japan restructured its trade agreements with foreign powers, eliminated the samurai class and feudal systems, modernized its infrastructure, imported technology and cultural knowledge from around the world, encouraged large-scale manufacturing and industry, promulgated a western-like constitution and a quasi-independent legislature, and more ominously for the region, got its first taste of becoming a colonial power. The Ryūkyū Kingdom—present-day Okinawa—had been a vassal state of Japan since the 1600s, but it was formally annexed in 1879, a minor transaction compared to what came next.

Japan was no stranger to mainland politics, having periodically extended its governance onto portions of the Korean peninsula over the centuries. With its new outlook and its shiny new western tools, it seemed natural to Japan that Korea should enact comparable upgrades. This had the side effect of making Korea less reliant on China, to which it had until recently been a vassal state. Disagreements over how much influence Japan and China should have on the Korean peninsula came to a head in the summer of 1894, when a minor revolt in Seoul escalated into a full-blown Sino-Japanese War. Nine months later, Japan emerged as the dominant power in the region, adding Taiwan and some other smaller islands to its collection, and bringing a newly independent Korean Empire into its sphere of influence.

Then there was Russia, which had worked to limit Japan's war spoils for its own purposes. Unbeknownst to Tōkyō, the Japanese Minister to Korea conspired to assassinate the pro-Russian Empress of Korea, initiating another conflict for regional control. Both sides suffered staggering losses in the Russo-Japanese War, but when the Battle of Tsushima brought a decisive end to the fight in 1905, Japan once again emerged on top, retaining control of Korea—eventually annexing the peninsula outright in 1910—and pushing the Russians out of Manchuria. By the time Emperor Meiji passed away in 1912, Japan had transitioned from a secluded, inward-looking island nation with residual seventeenth century sensibilities, into a modern military and industrial powerhouse that was fully comfortable reaching deep into the Asian landmass.

Warring States on an International Scale

Whether it was the *bushidō* samurai attitude that seeped into Japan's military ranks or some special blessing from Amaterasu herself, clearly something was going on with Japan. At least that is how it looked to the country's leadership. As Emperor Taishō ascended the throne, this sense of Japan's distinctiveness, this essence of national character, this *kokutai*, become official policy. Kokutai incorporated Confucian principles, a preference for consensus and harmony, and a respect for hierarchy and traditional culture into a program that merged the sacred and the secular. At its core stood the imperial line, instituted by the will of the sun goddess and therefore divine in nature, a nationalism clothed in state Shinto regalia. To revere the emperor—and by extension, his government and its growing martial elements—this defined a patriotic citizen.

This worldview guided Japan into the middle of the twentieth century, starting from The Great War. Japan played a minimal role in the conflict, but enough to share in the spoils, picking up German colonies in China and the North Pacific. The Great Kantō Earthquake of 1923, which destroyed the capital and killed over 100,000 residents, tempered national progress, and provided a moment of soul-searching. But what some of those souls found bordered on the radical, and various factions in Japan began flirting with the fascist, communist, and ultranationalist ideas that infected the world between the wars. There were even a few high-level assassinations and an attempted *coup d'état*. Eventually, the nationalist strain prevailed, not surprising given how well it aligned with the kokutai mindset. Textbooks touting the pro-empire philosophy entered the school system, backed up by anti-sedition laws and a societal elevation of the military.

For its most passionate adherents, Japan's special qualities couldn't be constrained to the islands. They needed room to stretch and grow, and there was no better place to start than with an invasion of Manchuria in 1931, which, once colonized, became a jumping off point for further expansion into China. This gave Japan access to vast agricultural and mineral resources needed for its post-earthquake economic health. Lest you think this was a power grab by a tyrant nation bent on world domination, Japan issued its vision for a "New Order in East Asia" through the "Greater East Asia Co-Prosperity Sphere," a partnership among Asian nations that would balance the western powers and bring economic independence to the East. And by "partnership," I mean that Japan would be in charge, an idea it cemented in 1940 by acquiring the nations of French Indochina recently vacated by Vichy France.

The western allies didn't think too much of this New Order. The United States, still officially a neutral player in World War II, worked to cut off Japan's supplies of oil, steel, and money, resources the empire needed to fulfill its goals. Seeing no point in further diplomacy, Prime Minister Tōjō Hideki and his government decided to use force as a means of settling this international dispute. On December 7, 1941, it launched an attack on America's naval forces based in Pearl Harbor, Hawaii.

Japan would extend its reach into Hong Kong, Thailand, Indonesia, the Philippines, and a swath of the South China Sea the following year, providing it with additional resources and manpower. But by waking a sleeping American giant, it initiated the conditions for the empire's downfall. A mere six months after the Hawaiian attack, the allies had already broken Japan's naval codes, giving them an edge that culminated in a victory at Midway Island that June, considered the turning point of the war's Pacific theater. Japan fought on for more than three years, but it finally surrendered to allied forces in mid-August 1945, days after the United States dropped atomic bombs on Hiroshima and Nagasaki.

Japan's Miraculous Post-War Resurgence

This wasn't a defeat; it was a humiliation. Millions of Japanese soldiers and civilians dead, cities in ruins, the economy in collapse, ordinary citizens living in hunger and despair. Allied soldiers roamed the streets, stripping the country of any remaining military authority and dignity. For Prime Minister Tōjō and six other top leaders: the gallows. And worst of all, Emperor Shōwa, a direct descendant of the gods, forced to humble himself before the victors, personally announcing on radio Japan's surrender—though stopping short of using the actual word. Cognizant of what lay ahead, the emperor's speech put the best spin on the worst of all outcomes, resolving "to pave the way for a grand peace for all the generations to come by enduring the unendurable and suffering what is insufferable."

That insufferable suffering was named Occupied Japan, a term appearing on manufactured goods of the era. For the first and only time in the island nation's history, it had to prostrate itself before foreigners. Douglas MacArthur, Supreme Commander of the Allied Powers, set up shop in the capital, his General Headquarters (GHQ) working to fulfill the terms of the Potsdam Declaration, provide short-term humanitarian aid, and rebuild political and social institutions, shredding anything that hinted at nationalism. Japan's new Constitution, crafted by foreigners in English, shifted sovereign authority from the now-mortal emperor to the people, and codified the promise that Japan would never again choose war.

And yet, though this thing called the Empire of Japan perished, Japan and its imperial line endured, even thrived. In 1952, the occupiers departed—mostly—and a miracle happened, a "modern economic miracle." Freed from the mandates of a military dictatorship, the country changed almost instantly into an industrial and financial behemoth. It was as if Oda Nobunaga rose again, his wave of military destruction working to unify the nation. Sony, a small electronics company opened just months after the surrender, released its first transistor radio in 1954, followed by the entire country releasing everything the world wanted. In the late 1980s, Japan surpassed the Soviet Union to become the second largest economy on earth.

Of course, it couldn't go on like this forever, especially with some Japanese investors making such poor decisions. In 1991, the nation's asset bubble collapsed, and Japan entered its "lost decades," where it wandered from one short-signed economic solution to another, thirsting for debt relief in a parched land of financial stagnation. This coincided with its paired aging-population and declining-birth-rate traumas, pushing it into a cycle of social decline that some believe has no end. Natural disasters have also tried to kick the nation when it is down, especially the 1995

Kōbe earthquake and the 2011 Tōhoku earthquake-tsunami-nuclear-meltdown triple disaster.

Nations have collapsed from just a subset of such troubles, but Japan never lost its composure. Its financial difficulties have persisted, but so has its position near the top of major economies, and worldwide hunger for its wares and culture never waned. The labor shortages and natural disasters are real, but so is the attention to detail and quality, making it an outlier in a world of cheap, plastic knockoffs and planned obsolescence. Incomes are stagnant compared to other Western powers, yet streets remain clean, crime is essentially nonexistent, and the idea of riots stemming from social instability is laughable.

This is where we find Japan today. If the history just reviewed is any indication, Japan will recover from its transitory concerns and endure, thanks in part to the constant endeavor of the people, but also to the unbroken imperial line. These days, the emperor is officially little more than a figurehead, but one that is linked to key cultural, social, and political institutions stretching back to Japan's foundations. It doesn't really matter whether that founding occurred in the heavens, or in 660 BC, or at the end of the Yayoi Period, since they each convey the sense of "always." Even when the emperor was powerless—especially when shoguns and regents ruled the nation—those in power lifted up the throne as a focal point for the move forward. This centrality of the monarch is even codified in modern law; Article 1 of the postwar Constitution declares, "The Emperor shall be the symbol of the State and of *the unity of the People*." (Emphasis added.) The mythos of the monarchy's origins and the temporal seat that came into being through it helped define and inform what Japan is through all its regnal generations.

CHAPTER TWO

Japan's Modern Constitution

A constitution defines the core principles of governance for a nation, a justification for that state's legal and political systems. Japan has had such defining principles going back to the Yamato Court era, but its first constitution in the modern sense came on the scene in 1889, enduring more than half a century before being replaced by Version 2.0, promulgated on November 3, 1946. This chapter offers a high-level overview of that current edition, but one has to ask: Why was it necessary to revamp something that was already fairly new?

World War II, that mid-century dustup, triggered a review of Japan's system of government. Yet the development of an updated post-war Constitution was not a *fait accompli*. The 1945 Potsdam Declaration that outlined the terms for Japan's surrender said, "The Japanese Government shall remove all obstacles to the revival and strengthening of democratic tendencies among the Japanese people," and perhaps it was possible to do that with only a few well-placed amendments. But General MacArthur's nation-building apparatus (GHQ) believed that larger, meaningful changes should be made or at least pondered, and the new document sprang from those expectations.

Updating the Constitution and Society Together

The current "Post-War Constitution" exists because of what happened in Japan under the earlier "Meiji Constitution," and a quick examination of the changes between them is essential to fully appreciate today's version. As a product of nineteenth-century wordsmiths, the Meiji Constitution uses that flowery, quasi-religious tone common at the time, something lost in its twentieth-century counterpart. But more importantly, the authority from which Japan's government carries out its duties changed dramatically in the post-war revision. Reading the documents together reveals four key structural updates that had major impacts on Japanese society.

1. **Source of sovereignty.** Under the 1889 Constitution, all sovereign authority rested with the emperor, not with any shogun who might care to show up, and certainly not with the people. Thanks to an imperial line "unbroken for ages eternal…, [the] Emperor is sacred and inviolable…combining in Himself the rights of sovereignty." The Meiji era introduced an elected legislature built along western lines, and that organ had reasonable constitutional powers. But the Meiji Constitution made it repeatedly clear that the emperor ruled the nation in

every respect. The preamble of the document is even written in his voice, filled with the royal "we declare" mandates of an ultimate potentate.

Today's Constitution fixes that authority with the Japanese people, and it is under their sovereign right that the Constitution exists at all. Lest there be any doubt, three of the preamble's four paragraphs start with, "We, the Japanese people…." This Enlightenment perspective would have been familiar to American Constitution buffs, including MacArthur and his GHQ team, but earlier drafts submitted by Japanese leadership also invoked this idea of popular sovereignty.

2. **Better separation of powers.** With the throne taking on a more symbolic role, the executive, legislative, and judicial branches became the primary instruments of governance. The new Constitution vested core power in the Diet, Japan's legislature, and the body closest to the sovereign people who elect its members. The new upper House of Councillors replaced the former House of Peers, supplanting imperial nobles loyal to the throne with members installed by direct popular election.

The executive power of the Cabinet proceeds from the Diet, but once established, a system of checks and balances keeps one side from dominating. The judiciary also provides a check on the legislative process, as courts retain the power of judicial review. Finally, the new Constitution strengthens provisions for regional and municipal government "in accordance with the principle of local autonomy."

3. **Civilian pacifist leadership.** Most residents of Japan know about Article 9, the constitutional clause wherein Japan renounces war as a means of solving its problems. It was a blunt, "don't you dare do that again" statement that codified a pacifist national outlook. But less familiar is a related addition in Article 66, demanding that, "The Prime Minister and other Ministers of State must be civilians." This eliminated the shogun-like tendency of having active military leaders—including war-time Prime Minister Tōjō Hideki—assume control over the government.

4. **Guarantee of civil rights.** The Meiji Constitution included coverage of civil rights, and the government of the era was to "respect and protect the security of the rights and of the property of Our people." But this expectation was subordinated to the emperor's sovereign prerogatives, descended as they did from heaven. For example, Article XXIX stated, "Japanese subjects shall *within the limits of law*, enjoy the liberty of speech, writing, publication,

public meetings, and associations." (Emphasis added.) That law was the law of the emperor, and similar language accompanied all the rights listed in that older document.

Under the new instrument, the people's fundamental human rights are "eternal and inviolable," and it is the government's role to secure those rights for this and future generations. Concerning those communication freedoms, the updated Constitution identifies them without qualification in Article 21: "Freedom of assembly and association as well as speech, press and all other forms of expression are guaranteed."

With that background settled, it's time to review the constitutional articles themselves. At around 5,000 words, the Japanese Constitution is one of the world's shortest, so it won't take long to cover the basics.

The Edict of Promulgation

The text of the document is often paired with the imperial edict signed by Emperor Shōwa. Although perhaps only interesting to nerds like me, the current Constitution became the supreme law of the land via an amendment process under the terms of the Meiji-era document. Article 73 of that older text provided the technical mechanism for updating the Constitution, and in his edict, the emperor announced that he did "hereby sanction and promulgate the

amendments of the Imperial Japanese Constitution"
according to the rules of Article 73.

The term "constitutional amendment" brings to mind
additions or targeted alterations to an existing contract. This
is the situation with America's Bill of Rights (its first ten
amendments), which upon passage became a unified part of
the core constitutional text. But in the case of Japan's post-
war update, the incoming verbiage replaced the earlier
version wholesale, thanks to a clause in the new document's
preamble that reads, "We reject and revoke all constitutions,
laws, ordinances, and rescripts in conflict herewith." By
issuing the new document this way, the nation of Japan and
its imperial line continued uninterrupted—what was
described at the time as "complete legal continuity with the
constitution of 1889"—albeit with significant adjustments
to guiding principles.

In addition to the emperor's seal, the edict was signed by
Prime Minister Yoshida Shigeru and fourteen other
ministers of state.

The Preamble

The post-war Constitution's introduction is all about the
people who, when stripped of their rights under previous
administrations, were "visited with the horrors of war
through the action of government." The term "people"
appears no less than ten times, eight of which refer to
Japan's body politic. After affirming that "sovereign power

resides with the people," the text waxes philosophical about their responsibilities: "Government is a sacred trust *of the people*, the authority for which is derived *from the people*, the powers of which are exercised by the representatives *of the people*, and the benefits of which are enjoyed *by the people*." (Emphasis added.)

Missing from this opening is any mention of the throne or its occupant. In fact, if you only looked at the preamble, you would have no idea that Japan is a constitutional monarchy. Instead of the people's relationship to the emperor, this intro plays up Japan's kinship with the rest of the world. The half-dozen references to other nations communicate a kumbaya sentimentality that is as idealistic as it is apologetic. The preamble's entire second paragraph is dedicated to restoring fraternal solidarity with other nations.

> We, the Japanese people, desire peace for all time and are deeply conscious of the high ideals controlling human relationship, and we have determined to preserve our security and existence, trusting in the justice and faith of the peace-loving peoples of the world. We desire to occupy an honored place in an international society striving for the preservation of peace, and the banishment of tyranny and slavery, oppression and intolerance for all time from the earth. We recognize that all peoples

> of the world have the right to live in peace, free from
> fear and want.

The remainder of this block expands on the moral philosophy that Japan will embrace going forward. America's founders appealed "to the Laws of Nature and of Nature's God" for its core principles. Japan's Constitution lacks such religious lingo, but instead assumes that the people already possess and can understand these *a priori* standards, since "laws of political morality are universal."

The text insists that "obedience to such laws is incumbent upon all nations." Is this a reminder to Japan itself to behave, or a call for other nations not to kick Japan while it is down? I honestly don't know, but by announcing the requirement of all sovereign nations to take responsibility for their interactions with others, the Constitution affirms emphatically that Japan is a sovereign nation, that its people have the right to promulgate this Constitution, and that it deserves a place on the world stage with other like-minded nations.

The Emperor

The Constitution groups its 103 articles into eleven chapters, the first of which focuses on the status of the emperor. The document's first mention of the monarch appears in Article 1.

> The Emperor shall be the symbol of the State and
> of the unity of the people, deriving his position

from the will of the people with whom resides
sovereign power.

Although the preamble was emphatic about the
sovereignty of the people, some readers may have already
forgotten, so Article 1 brings it up again. Formerly in a
position to bequeath all rights to the people, the emperor has
now transitioned to a "symbol of the State and the unity of
the people," a move decided and instituted by those same
people. It feels like a major downgrade moving from
sovereign to symbol, and Diet members reviewing drafts of
the text in 1946 grumbled that this update would harm
Japan's national character. Yet admiration for the emperor
has not lagged since the war, but has been consistently high.
One analysis found that just over half the citizenry approved
of the emperor in the early 1950s, a rating that had risen to
75 percent by the end of that decade, a level that endures to
this day.

The emperor used to be the final word on all functions of
government, but this chapter takes an enumerated approach,
listing the monarch's specific roles and activities, reserving
all other responsibilities to the people or the branches of
government to be defined later. Even then, "the advice and
approval of the Cabinet shall be required for all acts of the
Emperor in matters of state." The "state" is the idealized
embodiment of the people, and the emperor has specific
functions as symbol of that state. (Some commentators

identify the emperor as Japan's head of state, though the Constitution is silent on this terminology, and others argue against it.) By contrast, "government" is the practical implementation of state functions, and the emperor has no defined role at this level by design.

A few of the emperor's duties feel like an exercise of government power, including his role in appointing the prime minister and chief judge of the Supreme Court. But even these are performed at the behest and direction of government organs. All other functions are ceremonial in nature and are done on behalf of the people with the approval of the Cabinet.

- The emperor officially announces laws, treaties, amendments to the Constitution, and similar official acts, including grants of clemency.
- He acts as national greeter by receiving foreign ambassadors, attesting to new cabinet ministers, and handing out state honors.
- He shows up to open and close sessions of the Diet and announces the general election of Diet members.

The throne is still dynastic, according to Article 2, and provisions for regency remain. Finally, "No property can be given to, or received by, the Imperial House," so don't even try.

Renunciation of War

With two world wars in the rearview mirror and the Soviets already making noises in Eurasia, the GHQ was adamant to prevent another major conflagration. The Constitution's second chapter, with its solitary Article 9, communicates that desire.

> Aspiring sincerely to an international peace based on justice and order, the Japanese people forever renounce war as a sovereign right of the nation and the threat or use of force as means of settling international disputes.
>
> In order to accomplish the aim of the preceding paragraph, land, sea, and air forces, as well as other war potential, will never be maintained. The right of belligerency of the state will not be recognized.

The text is based in part on the "MacArthur Notes," a short memorandum that the general issued in February 1946, listing the three key constitutional imperatives. (The other two "musts" were retaining the emperor as head of state and eliminating the peerage system.) In that missive, Japan would not have anything resembling a military, "even for preserving its own security."

And yet, Japan has a military, its Self-Defense Forces, the fourth most powerful security service in the world by some accounts, one that includes submarines and aircraft carriers. This is not a new development; despite MacArthur's concerns over an equipped Japan, he kept its soldiers around, even having Japan's "National Police" take an active role on the Korean peninsula, where a new war against communism was ramping up.

In recent years, political leaders—especially the late prime minister Abe Shinzō—have attempted to define the country's right to self-defense at the constitutional level, passing an amendment that would state specifically this standard of military preparation. But even this nod to the current status quo has been a hard sell. Despite having a sizable, modernized force, Japan has grown comfortable with its pacifist moniker. A 2005 report by the Diet's House of Councillors confirmed that, "The Japanese people, with their experiences of the horror of the war, feel deeply attached to [pacifism]." That may be changing, though, thanks to China's military expansion over the past few decades, and Russia's 2022 invasion of Ukraine. While Japan shows no willingness to develop a martial force with offensive capabilities, there are signs of increasing comfort with a constitutionally defined defense organization.

Rights and Duties of the People

Chapter III, one of the largest blocks within the document, itemizes the civil rights and responsibilities of the Japanese people. Article 11 conveys the central Enlightenment principle that governments exist to protect the rights of the sovereign people.

> The people shall not be prevented from enjoying any of the fundamental human rights. These fundamental human rights guaranteed to the people by this Constitution shall be conferred upon the people of this and future generations as eternal and inviolate rights.

The influence of America's core founding documents on this chapter is obvious; the "life, liberty, and the pursuit of happiness" clause in Article 13 is lifted verbatim from the 1776 Declaration of Independence. Most of the core guarantees from the US Bill of Rights appear here, as do the equal-protection expectations from the post-Civil War Fourteenth Amendment, coincidentally appearing as Article 14.

> All of the people are equal under the law and there shall be no discrimination in political, economic or social relations because of race, creed, sex, social status or family origin.

The enumerated rights included in the Japanese Constitution are legion: freedom of thought, conscience, speech, and assembly; freedom of religion; universal adult suffrage for the selection of representatives; property rights; the right to petition the government for redress of damages; the right to unionize and bargain collectively; access to due process and a writ of *habeas corpus*; freedom from unreasonable search and seizure; the guarantee of a fair and speedy trial (albeit one without a jury of peers); the right to legal counsel; protection from self-incrimination, *ex post facto* prosecution, and double jeopardy; freedom of movement in residence and employment; and on and on and on.

In addition to civil and political rights, the current Constitution also invokes social rights, including "the right to maintain the minimum standards of wholesome and cultured living" (Article 25). The document also weighs in on marriage, with Article 24 reminding the public that "it shall be based only on the mutual consent of both sexes and it shall be maintained through mutual cooperation with the equal rights of husband and wife as a basis." Then there is Article 23, a short entry that guarantees academic freedom.

Beyond the mention of various rights, Chapter III spends a lot of ink documenting the duties and responsibilities of the people, something only hinted at in the American counterpart. Article 12 lays out the expectation that the people, sovereign as they are, cannot simply take their rights for granted, but must be vigilant in protecting them.

> The freedoms and rights guaranteed to the people by this Constitution shall be maintained by the constant endeavor of the people, who shall refrain from any abuse of these freedoms and rights and shall always be responsible for utilizing them for the public welfare.

To that end, the people have not only the right to work, but the obligation to do so (Article 27). And that work will likely be taxed, another responsibility of the people (Article 30). In general, despite the natural rights inherent in each person, the Constitution makes it clear that they can only be invoked within community limits, and that this self-restraint is a duty that goes hand-in-hand with possessing rights in the first place. Article 13 binds rights and duties together in one compound expectation.

> [The people's] right to life, liberty, and the pursuit of happiness shall, *to the extent that it does not interfere with the public welfare*, be the supreme consideration in legislation and in other governmental affairs. (Emphasis added.)

Article 22, the entry that guarantees freedom of employment and movement of residence, likewise adds the restrictive "to the extent that it does not interfere with the public welfare" clause to the natural right, a reminder of the high value that Japan places on social harmony.

The Diet

The Diet is Japan's national legislative body and, according to Article 41, "the highest organ of state power." While cabinet ministers in the executive branch and judges at all levels of the judiciary are selected by other, more indirect means, legislators are chosen by a direct vote of the people and are, in theory, the government officials who most closely represent the will of the people. In terms of authority, this puts them at a higher level than the prime minister, even higher than the emperor himself. Yet the people are still sovereign and could chuck the Diet and the entire system of government if things ever became tyrannical.

Despite the excitement that people have when discussing the rights secured through modern constitutions, the bulk of these legal contracts contain boring descriptions of organizations and systems, and the sections covering the Diet, the Cabinet, and the Supreme Court are as mundane as you can possibly imagine. I plan on discussing the functions and interactions of these three branches in a later chapter, so I won't be repeating those details here. But a quick summary of how the Diet is crafted constitutionally is in order.

Structurally, the Diet is bicameral, consisting of an upper House of Councillors with members elected to six-year terms, and a lower House of Representatives with members elected to four-year terms. Despite the positional label, anytime the two houses can't agree on the content of a bill, the lower house can override the House of Councillors. Yet when the prime minister decides to dissolve the legislature early, it is the members of the House of Representatives who lose their jobs; the upper house merely goes into recess.

Once each year (currently in January), both houses begin their annual Ordinary Session. After this session ends or if the House of Representatives has been dissolved, an *ad hoc* Extraordinary Session can be called during emergencies. Finally, a Special Session is called when it comes time to select a new prime minister after an election. In all cases, a quorum of one-third of members is required for either house to conduct business, and by default all decisions are by majority vote. In most cases, sessions are open to the public.

I would never say that legislators are more prone to crime that ordinary citizens, but Article 50 says that members of either house cannot be arrested when the Diet is in session, and if an elected member is already in jail—not that they would be—they must be released while the legislature is in session.

One reason the Japanese Constitution is so much shorter than others is that it left many details to be decided later. Just in this chapter covering the Diet, there are four significant details that were to be "fixed by law" at some future point: the number of Diet members in each house; electoral qualification for members, including minimum age; election details such as voting methods and the makeup of electoral districts; and the impeachment process for judges.

The Cabinet

The Cabinet carries out the executive functions of the state. It consists of a prime minister (always a current Diet member) and other ministers of state (most of whom must be current Diet members); they must all be civilians. Anytime there is an election, or if the Cabinet has been dissolved, a new Cabinet is built again from scratch. Here are the basic steps.

1. The Diet calls for a Special Session.
2. In that session, the Diet selects a prime minister from its own members. If the two houses can't agree, the House of Representatives gets to decide.
3. If the previous Cabinet was still active and working on, you know, Cabinet stuff, all its members will immediately resign *en masse*.
4. The incoming prime minister selects the members of the new Cabinet, the various ministers of state. The PM can also fire any of these ministers at any time, and for any reason.
5. Later, if the House of Representatives isn't pleased with the Cabinet, it can perform a no-confidence vote. If that passes, the Cabinet must resign *en masse* and the whole process starts again.

As someone who grew up in America with its strong commitment to the separation of powers, the relationship between the Diet and the Cabinet feels extremely chummy. The Diet selects the prime minister, and most Cabinet ministers must also be current Diet members. Article 66 says, "The Cabinet is collectively responsible to the Diet." But the Cabinet is also given a modicum of power over the Diet, as the prime minister can, at any time, dissolve the House of Representatives and call for a new election. (The

House of Councillors cannot be dissolved.) Talk about ingratitude.

If the United States had some of these features, I could see the no-confidence votes and house dissolutions happening on a weekly basis, and nothing would ever get done. But it all seems to work in Japan. Speaking of work, here is what the Cabinet does.

- Submits budgets, treaties, and other bills to the Diet for approval.
- As the executive, manages foreign and domestic affairs.
- Oversees the various administrative branches and submits related reports to the Diet.
- Issues cabinet orders, regulatory instructions needed to carry out laws.
- Grants amnesty, commutations, and other reprieves from incarceration.

The prime minister and the relevant minister of state must also sign each law and cabinet order. This is a requirement; the Cabinet has no veto power over the legislature.

The Judiciary

Of the three main branches of government, the judiciary is the most independent, by which I mean it is the one most distant (by design) from the people and from the other branches. It is true that the Cabinet chooses who sits on the

Supreme Court, and the emperor appoints that court's chief judge from Cabinet recommendations. But once seated, it's mostly hands off. Impeachment or removal for mental or physical incompetency is possible but rare. Still, the people in their sovereign role have a say once every ten years, voting to retain or dismiss each sitting judge, something not even the American system allows at the national level.

The Constitution designates a Supreme Court with a chief judge and "such number of judges as may be determined by law" (Article 79). It also authorizes a system of "inferior courts as are established by law" (Article 76). This Supreme Court, once constituted, has almost unrestricted say in how the judicial branch operates. It sets "all rules and practices" for itself, all lower courts, attorneys, and prosecutors. The legislature sets the number and place of inferior courts, but its ranks are filled by Supreme Court nominees subsequently appointed by the Cabinet for ten-year terms.

Since the Supreme Court has so much authority in crafting the judicial branch, there isn't much more to glean from the Constitution other than these two features: With specific exceptions, all trials are to be conducted publicly; and judges must be paid a regular salary that, once set, can never be lowered.

Finance

The Japanese government collects taxes and spends that money on stuff, lots of stuff it turns out, and the executive and legislative branches get together to determine how it happens. According to Chapter VII of the Constitution, the Cabinet submits a budget to the Diet, which thinks about it for a while and then decides what can be spent. Article 87 does provide the Cabinet with a reserve fund for use in emergencies, but the Diet gets a say on how it is used.

The document is mostly silent on how the government spends its money, but it does include one specific restriction in Article 89: "No public money or other property shall be expended or appropriated for the use, benefit or maintenance of any religious institution or association, or for any charitable, educational or benevolent enterprises not under the control of public authority."

Article 88 provides another reminder that the emperor is no longer officially in charge. It says that the Imperial Household—the apparatus surrounding the emperor—can't own anything. Rather, imperial property "belongs to the state," and the Diet must approve any expenses by the Imperial Household.

Finally, all spending is audited annually by a Board of Audit, and every year the Cabinet must report "to the Diet and the people on the state of national finances."

Local Self-Government

Chapter VIII includes four articles that define the need for "local public entities…in accordance with the principle of local autonomy." These local jurisdictions—prefectures, cities, and so on—have their own executive and legislative branches that can establish and enforce their own regulations. The Diet can pass laws for these jurisdictions as well, but they will be one-size-fits-all edicts. If the national legislature does pass a custom law just for one local area, it must also be approved by a majority of voters in that region.

Amendments

The people of Japan, through their legislature, can amend the Constitution. Such amendments must be passed by a two-thirds vote of the Diet followed by a majority vote of the people. Once passed, the emperor promulgates the ratified change, and it becomes a fixed part of the full constitutional text.

This has yet to happen, making Japan's untouched Constitution an outlier in a world where politicians love to tinker with foundational laws. It's not for lack of trying. Prime Minister Abe Shinzō attempted to revise Article 9—the renunciation-of-war section—all throughout his premiership to clarify the status of Japan's defense corps. In 2000, the Diet commissioned an examination into ways that the Constitution could be adapted for modern realities, although the final report that came out five years later said little more than, "Let's do this again sometime." Even if it had put concrete changes to a vote, there is scant public desire for modifying the document. Since a majority vote of the people is a requirement for revising the Constitution, a revamping of how the public views its core document must come first before any successful amendment process.

Supreme Law

Before establishing the authority of the Constitution, this penultimate chapter gets philosophical about natural rights and the human struggle to secure them, reinforcing in Article 97 some of the ideas from the preamble: "The fundamental human rights by this Constitution guaranteed to the people of Japan are fruits of the age-old struggle of man to be free; they have survived the many exacting tests for durability and are conferred upon this and future generations in trust, to be held for all time inviolate."

With that out of the way, this self-referential block declares that the Constitution is the supreme law of Japan, and any law, ordinance, imperial rescript, or act of government that conflicts with it is invalid. "The Emperor or the Regent as well as Ministers of State, members of the Diet, judges, and all other public officials have the obligation to respect and uphold this Constitution."

Supplementary Provisions

The last four articles deal with housekeeping issues needed for the initial transition from the Meiji Constitution to this new edition, akin to backing up your files when upgrading to a new computer. Most of these have to do with the continuity of government officials already serving during the changeover. Article 100 also allowed the old Diet to get a head start, voting on any laws needed to carry out the mandates of the new Constitution even before it takes effect.

This section stipulated that the new Constitution would become active six months after promulgation. With Emperor Shōwa announcing the change on November 3, 1946, the new version went live on May 3, 1947. Both dates are now public holidays: Constitution Memorial Day occurs on May 3 each year, followed by Culture Day in November. Since former Emperor Meiji's birthday was celebrated on November 3 until his passing in mid-1912, the promulgation date was likely not a coincidence. The former Meiji Constitution had been promulgated on February 11, which, when adjusted for calendar changes, points to the lunisolar New Year's Day, and commemorates the day that, by tradition, Emperor Jimmu became the nation's first monarch in 660 BC.

CHAPTER THREE

State Symbols of Japan

Symbols, whether official or de facto, are part of a society's atmosphere, blending almost unnoticeably with the nitrogen and oxygen that everyone breathes. Even if citizens never think about them, they know these intrinsic totems and associate them with what it means to be Japanese.

This chapter introduces key symbols embraced by Japanese citizens. Some of them are composed of words and expressions, others are images; one is a person. Regardless of the makeup, they offer insights into Japanese culture's inner workings, and understanding the symbols, including how they work at a subconscious level, can help immigrants better mesh with the native population.

National Name

The two characters of Japan's national name, 日本 (*Nihon* or *Nippon*), are about as simple as a country name can get. The formal name is 日本国 (*Nihon-koku*), usually translated as "State of Japan," but even official documents use the more common two-character version. Most of Japan's neighbors have names that make a political statement about their representative forms of government, accurate or not: Republic of Korea, People's Republic of China, Socialist Republic of Vietnam, Republic of the Philippines, and so on. Using this pattern, perhaps the country's name should be, "Monarchy of Japan with Constitutional Limits that Make it Function More Like a Parliamentary Republic." But why write all that when "Japan" says it all?

Before World War II, the nation was known as 大日本帝国 (*Dai-Nihon-teikoku*). Officially, the English translation was "Empire of Japan," but with that initial 大 character, meaning "great" or "large," it is not surprising that Japan viewed itself as a Great Empire ready to expand its reach. That wasn't the first time that Japan changed its name into something grand. Back in the Yamato era, some Chinese mainlanders took to calling the island nation 倭 (*wa*), meaning "distant," or worse, "submissive." Locals replaced this quasi-slur with 和 (also *wa*), later prefixing it with "great" to become 大和, pronounced *Yamato* and literally meaning "great harmony." Even in those earliest societal moments, the nation treated its name as an important symbol of its core identity.

Japan's current moniker is also defined with symbolic identity in mind. The characters that form the name 日本 mean "sun" and "foundation," respectively. Or, to put it another way, Japan is the "Land of the Rising Sun." As a youth in America, I always assumed this was nothing more than a convenient link to Japan's proximity to the International Date Line. But when your nation's source of authority is none other than the sun goddess herself, it is a small step to self-identification with the origin of each day's solar transit. With every new sunrise, Japan's *raison d'être* is renewed, and the country's chosen moniker is a reminder to its citizens and the world of this hallowed identity.

The Emperor

As we saw in the previous chapter, Japan's modern Constitution identifies the emperor as a "symbol of the State." Although his role as Japan's head of state is highly limited and strictly defined, the status of 天皇 (*ten'nō*, "Emperor of Heaven") as a symbol is quite broad and not always easy to pin down.

By tradition, Japan's current royal line stretches back to 660 BC when Jimmu became the first emperor. The various shoguns sucked a lot of the power out of the throne, and that entire Northern-Southern Court thing during the 1300s made imperial recordkeeping a fair mess. And yet, Japan's official policy is that the imperial line has remained secure, unbroken, and sovereign since its founding. Even when it functioned nominally under military governments, the monarch was viewed as the focal point for national authority. This has the effect of tethering the Chrysanthemum Throne to the entire history of Japan, and to everything that defined Japan at each moment along that timeline.

Because of the legendary connection between the sitting monarch and the goddess Amaterasu, the symbolism of the emperor extends theoretically into heaven itself, far beyond the nation's watery borders. Does this mean that everyone in Japan accepts the creation myth from the *Nihon Shoki* as historical fact, or that the emperor has some mystical superpower that binds the nation together? Of course not. But if we glance once more at that line from the Constitution, we find that it identifies the emperor as "the symbol of the State *and of the unity of the people*." (Emphasis added.) There is something in this world called "the unity of the Japanese people." It's not easy to determine what binds tens of millions of people together, but however the phrase is defined, the sovereign Japanese people have decided to manifest this unity symbolically in the person of the emperor. There are a few Japanese citizens who have called for the abolition of the monarchy, it is true. But overall, a general sense of national solidarity exists in Japan; it is recognized as having roots in the country's history and traditions; and public opinion surveys affirm that the people see the emperor as a successful symbol of that kinship.

Still, one can't sit around being a symbol all day long. That's why the emperor's job description includes various ceremonial and state functions. He meets important people when the need arises, from foreign ambassadors to residents suffering a natural disaster. His duties also bring gravitas and significance to otherwise standard government functions: He presides over the opening of the annual Diet session, appoints the prime minister and chief judge of the Supreme Court, promulgates all laws and treaties, and confers national honors.

Having a monarch as head of state who is distinct from the branches of government may also provide a tempering influence on political excesses. A politician who behaves badly may have no problem dispensing with his own conscience and pay lip service to the general public. But the knowledge that there is a personification of the state in residence just a few blocks away from the seat of government, and that misdeeds would reflect poorly not only on the nation, but on the beloved, heaven-linked symbol of that nation may provide just one more check against such violations of the public trust. From a human-behavior perspective, it is surely easier for an elected official to uphold the dignity of a kindly, revered monarch than it is to lend that same level of respect to over 100 million faceless, nameless citizens.

The Imperial Seal

Japan is an emblem-based society. If you have ever touched a piece of paper in Japan, it more than likely had a seal on it, an orangish stamp that identifies a person or organization. A step above these verification stamps are the *mon* and *kamon*, idiographic logos linked with individuals, families, or organizations. You might see such glyphs on a corporate building or the flag of a warrior clan, where they identify the property or presence of anyone associated with that symbol.

At the tippy top of the *mon* hierarchy is the Imperial Seal of Japan, historically used only by the Imperial Household to mark its stuff. These days, usage is more flexible, but you still can't register a trademark that contains it as it is designated for official use.

Thanks in part to the north-south court split so many centuries ago, there are a few different seal formats. The most common is the yellow sixteen-leaf chrysanthemum, one of those simple-yet-elegant images that artists are always suffering for. This familiar emblem appears on all Japanese passports, the emperor's throne, and on any gift or proclamation issued from the Imperial Household (Figure 3-1).

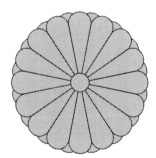

Figure 3-1. The Imperial Seal of Japan.

Because of its association with the emperor, the seal isn't something that people necessarily interact with or see on a daily basis. But when it does come into view, there is an automatic recollection that this is something that means Japan.

There are other seals that are used by the government to mark or validate its property or management. Some of them are traditional inked stamps that, while present on all kinds of official documents that people have seen, are far from memorable. The national government also has a logo that it displays at press conferences, in foreign embassies, at the prime minister's office, and so on. It is fauna-centric, displaying Japan's favorite paulownia tree with a 5-7-5 leaf pattern, the same counts found in haiku poetry (Figure 3-2).

Figure 3-2. The Government Seal of Japan.

The Flag

Japan's national flag is called the 日の丸 (*hinomaru*), and like so many names in Japan, the term states exactly what it is:

"the ball of the sun." A large crimson circle set on a white field, Japan's flag is one of the most recognizable emblems in the world (Figure 3-3). And so easy to draw. As a kid, it would take me forever to add all fifty stars and thirteen stripes to Old Glory, but if you have enough red crayons, you can easily whip out a Japanese flag in under a minute.

Figure 3-3. The Flag of Japan.

There is another version of the flag that adds sunbeams, sometimes called the "Rising Sun Flag." Still in use by Japan's Self-Defense Forces, this variant's association with military exploits invokes memories of the pre-war, adversarial Empire of Japan, especially in the minds of regional powers.

Because of this link, and because nationalism and flag-waving often work in tandem, displays of any Japanese flag are less common that you might experience with, say, Britain's Union Jack. But it does show up at government facilities and on national holidays, and I have seen it more and more on televised sporting events, where fans wave the *hinomaru* to encourage their favorite Japanese sports heroes.

Neither the flag nor the national anthem (discussed below) had official standing until passage of the Act on

National Flag and Anthem, in 1999. Although this terse law did little more than provide rubber-stamp approval to two symbols already in common use by both government and the public, worries about a return to nationalism nearly prevented passage of an otherwise mundane act of the legislature. For all you graphic-design geeks, check out the appendices to the law, which provide the exact measurements and color codes for the flag's central ball.

The Anthem

Maxing out at just thirty-two words, Japan's national anthem, *Kimi ga yo*, is the world's shortest. The song's text derives from a tenth-century Heian poem, its archaic words and forms as mysterious as a Shakespearean sonnet is to modern English readers. The official text includes just five short lines.

君が代は *(kimigayo wa)*

千代に八千代に *(chiyo ni yachiyo ni)*

さざれ石の *(sazare-ishi no)*

巌となりて *(iwao to narite)*

苔の生すまで *(koke no musu made)*

I offer here a translation of my own design, for your consideration.

> May your era endure
> For a thousand, no, for eight thousand generations
> Until tiny pebbles
> Grow into boulders
> Covered with moss

As with the flag, controversy abounded when the government placed its imprimatur on this anthem. It's all due to the verse's opening character, 君 (*Kimi*), often translated these days as "you." Who is this "you" people keep singing about? By most accounts, it is the emperor, which prompts some to ask what people were doing in his name in the run-up to World War II. Others insist that the term is a stand-in for Japan in general, though this position is more difficult to justify. Since these days the emperor is the official symbol of Japan, the modern understanding could very well be a mixture of these two arguments, where *Kimi* is in fact the emperor, but only to the extent that he is a symbol for Japan itself.

A year into Emperor Meiji's reign, when Japan was embracing all things Western, the ancient text received a musical upgrade via a hip new tune, composed by John William Fenton, an Irish musician working as a military band leader for a British regiment then based in Yokohama. Far from eight thousand generations, the tune lasted just a decade before giving way to an even newer edition in 1880. Japanese court composer Hayashi Hiromori—or possibly his aides Oku Yoshiisa and Hayashi Akimori—and German composer Franz Eckert joined forces to produce the music still in use today, a decidedly Japanese melody overlaid with western harmonies.

National Holidays

Japan has *a lot* of official holidays, a full sixteen at last count. And here they are.

- January 1 is New Year's Day (*ganjitsu*), the focal point for a series of overlapping celebrations that all point to new beginnings. The entire year-end, year-start season is called *nen-matsu nen-shi*, split into a year-end portion called *toshi no se* and a year-start portion called *toshi ake*. Many people take off from work during this festive time, most often from December 29 through January 3.

  Here is where the names start to build up. New Year's Eve itself is known as *ōmisoka*, followed by *gantan*, the first morning of the new year. This is also the start of *shōgatsu*, which comes in 1-day, 3-day, 7-day, and all-January variations depending on how the term is used. You can also apply the word *sanga-nichi* to the first three days of the year, a time when people engage in *hatsumōde*, the first visit of the year to a Shinto shrine. When the holiday is over, it's time to return to work, a task known as *shigoto hajime* or *goyō hajime*.

- The second Monday in January is Coming of Age Day (*sei'nen no hi*). It is a time to celebrate youth, specifically those who turned eighteen between the previous April 2 and the upcoming April 1. Before 2022, the boundary was at age twenty, and some communities still use that as the cut-off. The celebrants get dressed up, especially the women who wear a special kimono called *furisode*.

- February 11 is National Foundation Day (*kenkoku kinen no hi*). This day commemorates the founding of Japan, traditionally linked to the ascension of Jimmu, Japan's first emperor, to the throne, in 660 BC.

- February 23 is the Emperor's Birthday (*ten'nō tanjyōbi*), although the date changes with each new monarch. Before the Reiwa era, this holiday fell on December 23, the birthday of Emperor Heisei. When Crown Prince Akishino ascends to the throne someday, this holiday will shift to November 30. Because the celebration date changes immediately upon a transition in emperor, you might get years where the holiday happens zero or two times.

- The annual Vernal Equinox (*shunbun no hi*) happens around March 20. This day is set aside for admiring nature with the kind of joy invoked by a bright new spring after a dark and cold winter.

- April 29 is Shōwa Day (*Shōwa no hi*). This date had been the birthday celebration of Emperor Shōwa up until his passing in 1989. As mentioned above, that holiday was switched to December 23 for Emperor Heisei, but that would have left a gap in the extremely popular string of holidays known as Golden Week. To keep the status quo, the government reinvented April 29 as Greenery Day. A further reshuffling of celebrations in 2007 converted this date to Shōwa Day, closer in spirit to its original purpose, and now the official start of Golden Week each year.

- May 3 is Constitution Day (*kenpō kinenbi*). Similar in tone to National Foundation Day, this springtime holiday commemorates the day that the new post-war Constitution came into effect in the late 1940s.

- May 4 is Greenery Day (*midori no hi*). Another day to exult in nature, this celebration moved from April 29 in 2007, perhaps to cement the idea that Golden Week is a festive, holiday-laden time of the year.

- May 5 is Children's Day (*kodomo no hi*). This date used to be called "Boy's Day"—the parallel "Girl's Day" was on March 3—and therefore it is common to see displays of miniature samurai gear on this day. Fish-shaped kites known as *koi nobori* also festoon streets

and shop windows. This holiday also marks the final
day of Golden Week.

- Marine Day (*umi no hi*) occurs on the third Monday
  in July. This is a newer holiday, created in the mid-
  1990s. It is the third nature-focused holiday of the
  year, but it won't be the last. This celebration used to
  fall on July 20, but it was moved to the third Monday
  of that month as part of the "Happy Monday"
  system, a law from the turn of the century that made
  permanent several three-day weekends throughout
  the year.

- August 11 is Mountain Day (*yama no hi*). This is the
  newest of the national holidays, established in 2014
  as yet another nature-related holiday. This day also
  overlaps with the many *Obon* festivals that occur
  throughout the country each mid-August, traditional
  Buddhist memorials for one's ancestors.

- The third Monday of September is Respect for the
  Aged Day (*keirō no hi*). It is a recently added holiday
  designed to celebrate life in general and the elderly in
  particular.

- The Autumnal Equinox (*shūbun no hi*) occurs around
  September 23 each year. This memorial is the fall
  counterpart to the springtime Vernal Equinox, and a
  reminder that we are reaching the end of the holiday
  list. Wow! So many!

- The second Monday in October is Sports Day (*supōtsu no hi*). Established just after the 1964 Tōkyō Olympics, this is a day to celebrate health and sportsmanship. The date jumped around for the 2020/2021 Olympiad, but it returned to its mid-October place after those ceremonies finished.

- November 3 is Culture Day (*bunka no hi*). This is the date of the modern Constitution's promulgation, and by an amazing coincidence it is also Emperor Meiji's birthday. The modern holiday celebrates culture, freedom, and peace, likely in equal measures.

- November 23 is Labor Thanksgiving Day (*kinrō kansha no hi*). It's not Labor Day; it's not Thanksgiving Day; it's both! Officially a secular holiday, this occasion hearkens back to a harvest festival celebrated in Japan long ago.

As if these official holidays were not enough, Japan also enjoys other less official annual memorials.

- Although they lack the legal sanction of their spring and fall equinoctial counterparts, the summer and winter solstices are just as traditional, taking place around the twentieth of June and December, respectively, each year.

- I mentioned a Girl's Day memorial on March 3 that got officially merged into the May 5 Children's Day holiday. The original day still exists, though, and is known as *hina matsuri*.

- *Tanabata* is a "Star Festival" that occurs on July 7 in some parts of Japan, August 7 in other regions. On this day, you will see people writing down wishes on strips of paper and hanging them from bamboo trees. Oftentimes, these wishes will have romantic undertones because of the religious legend on which this holiday is based.

- *Tsukimi*, which literally means "seeing the moon," is a mid-Autumn celebration of the full moon. Typically taking place in September or October, these days it is commonly celebrated by buying hamburgers and other fast-food items that have sunny-side-up eggs on them.

- *Shichi-go-san* means "seven, five, three," and the mid-November event celebrates three- and seven-year-old girls and five-year-old boys. Kids dress up in traditional kimonos and take formal photos.

- Holidays are so popular in Japan that even foreign celebrations make the list. Christmas (December 25) and Halloween (October 31) are big deals here, and while they lack the core religious sentiments, they make up for it in decorating fervor. These transplants are not official holidays, so people still need to go to work and school.

- Valentine's Day (February 14) is another import, a day when women traditionally give chocolates to men. Don't worry about unrequited love: White Day occurs on March 14, when men return the favor.

What are we to make of all these holidays? Japan has a reputation for being a hard-working country, where employees stay at their desks late into the evening, sometimes to the point of *karōshi* ("death by overwork"). And yet, the country has an above-average number of days off.

The holidays differ in focus and origin, but they all serve as symbols of Japan, and as such have a unifying effect on the populace. This is true even for the imported celebrations; the entire nation of Japan rushes out to buy fried chicken and strawberry shortcake on Christmas. Many of the holidays stem from centuries-old religious or political events that brought communities together to celebrate.

Our modern, technology-laden lives have reduced the communal impacts of these memorials, at least on an official level, but they still invoke the unity of the Japanese people. And you don't need to be a Japanese citizen to join in the festivities. Although we were living in America at the time, my own son dressed up in a kimono on his fifth birthday and had formal *shichi-go-san* photographs taken. He barely remembers it, and yet it has joined him symbolically to elements of his Japanese heritage going back to the nation's founding.

Imperial Regalia

Emperors have a normal human lifespan, and each monarch's obligation to stand as a national symbol is momentary when measured against the full arc of Japanese history. To effect passage of that symbolic role from one ruler to the next, Japan retains Three Sacred Treasures (*sanshu no jingi*), holy relics that are ceremonially linked to the imperial throne as the official Imperial Regalia of Japan.

Hidden from the public and stored separately in three different locations, they are brought together once each regnal generation as part of the emperor's enthronement rites. According to legend, these objects were gifted by the sun goddess Amaterasu to her grandson, Ninigi-no-Mikoto, who subsequently passed them on to his own grandson Jimmu, Japan's first ruler. These treasures are physical objects that convey three core virtues from one generation to the next.

- The sword *Kusanagi no Tsurugi* represents valor. As with the other two relics, its exact storage location is a guarded secret, but the consensus is that it is housed at the Atsuta Shrine in Nagoya.
- The mirror *Yata no Kagami* represents wisdom. This item is believed to be near the sitting emperor, stored on the grounds of the Imperial Palace in Tōkyō.

- The jewel *Yasakani no Magatama* represents benevolence. If the rumors be true, it is stored at the Ise Grand Shrine in Mie Prefecture.

Court records show these tokens being used during the emperor's ascent to the throne as far back as the seventh century, although there is much scholarly debate as to whether the items used today are facsimiles for relics that may have been lost during Japan's many periods of upheaval. Original or not, they are treated as holy, and it is reported that even the current emperor has never laid eyes on them, as they are shrouded from view during the secret ceremonies. This adds to their allure as mysterious symbols of the nation.

Other Symbols

Japan has other objects that, while lacking the official standing of each symbol listed above, perform a similar function in uniting the Japanese people. And there is no unofficial token more well known than Mount Fuji. Still an active volcano, this natural facet of Japan is recognized internationally as a placeholder for the entire nation.

On clear days, I can see the tippy top of Mount Fuji from my Tōkyō-area office. It is hard to put into words, but catching a glimpse of its snowy peak stirs the heart. Even though it is a common sight, if you mention to someone that you saw the mountain earlier in the day, the response is often an excited "Really!?" The Japanese people *love* Mount

Fuji, consistently, universally, unendingly. As a symbol, it is dripping with clues that are meant to invoke an understanding of Japan itself: majestic, stately, orderly, long-lasting. In some ways, it is Japan, and while that can't possibly be accurate, it still provides a symbolic glue that brings the country's people into a union of sorts.

Various flora and fauna also act as stand-ins for the nation. In the animal kingdom, the red-crowned crane (*tanchōzuru*) is a familiar site, perhaps most famously as the logo for Japan Airlines. The green pheasant (*kiji*) is the national bird of Japan and a native to the archipelago. *Nishikigoi*, commonly known as *koi*, is a colorful carp admired worldwide as a familiar emblem of Japan.

In the plant world, chrysanthemums (*kiku*) are an obvious symbol, given their link to the royal household. But their fame is eclipsed by cherry trees (*sakura*), their annual blooms attracting millions of domestic and international tourists. Finally, the paulownia tree (*kiri*) is a popular wood product used in building traditional *tansu* cabinets. The Japanese government's official seal consists primarily of a flowering paulownia.

You don't need to be part of the tree of life to be a symbol of Japan. Some of the more enduring castles, shrines, temples, and even hot springs spread throughout the country act as national or regional symbols, embodying the history, traditions, and core beliefs of Japan. Activities can also exist as symbols of the nation, including sumo, karate, and shogi. And then there's the food.

Japan is not alone in hosting a variety of national objects and activities that bring a particular nation to mind. England has a constitutional monarch who plays a role akin Japan's emperor. China has its Twelve Ornaments that collectively symbolize aspects of Chinese tradition. France has its many cheeses and Bordeaux wines. The *Dia de los Muertos* is a Mexican holiday that has symbology drawn from seemingly unrelated historical realities. And yet, there is something about the symbology of Japan that causes people to stop and think, "Wow, that is so Japanese!"

CHAPTER FOUR

How Japan's Government Works

A chapter title like "How Government Works" is begging for an hour of stand-up jokes. But as this is a civics book and not a nightclub, let's jump right into learning about Japan's administrative state. As you recall from Chapter 2, the basic structure of the Japanese government is defined through the text of its national Constitution. But that short document provides just the essentials, describing the bare minimum for the legislative, executive, and judicial branches of government. The day-to-day functioning of public systems requires a body of laws, rules, traditions, and social dynamics. In Japan, some of those were developed in tandem with the current Constitution while others transitioned over from the Meiji era.

In this chapter, we'll focus less on constitutional theory and instead look at the functions of governance as experienced by the people. The terse nature of the Constitution, its demand that some details be implemented through post-promulgation laws, and its deferral to regional and municipal governments on local matters mean that much of what passes for government came about through extra-constitutional processes. I'm not going to list out the text of any laws here—sorry to dash your hopes. Instead, this chapter will summarize the practical functions of government which residents, citizens or otherwise, encounter through news reports and visits to city hall.

Try as you might, you won't find a distinct section in this chapter on the emperor. That's because Japan's monarch has no official government function. It is true that he performs some ceremonial activities that feel like government acts: convoking the Diet, promulgating laws and treaties, dissolving the House of Representatives, receiving foreign ambassadors and other dignitaries, and more. But all these tasks are done at the direction of and under the purview of the Diet or the Cabinet. By himself, the emperor has no actual government power, but only presents a similitude of governmental authority thanks to his role as a symbol of the state. In this way, he is like a ray of symbolic sunshine falling on the constitutional edifice of the three branches as crafted by the sovereign people.

The Diet

When I first moved to Japan and started vegging out in front of the TV, I was surprised at how much airtime the Diet— the national bicameral legislature—received. Back in America, you might see the halls of Congress during the annual State of the Union address, assuming a rerun of *Seinfeld* wasn't available on another channel. But here in

Japan, televised floor speeches by politicians are a near-daily feature of broadcast news or above-the-fold journalism. This includes comments by the prime minister who, though the official presiding over the executive branch, is by constitutional mandate an elected member of the Diet.

This is how it should be. While Japan has separation of powers into three distinct legislative, executive, and judicial branches, the Diet is by far "the highest organ of state power." It is also the only one chosen by a direct vote of the sovereign people from whom the government acquires its authority. Regular press coverage of the goings on of congressional leaders provides at least the façade of responsibility to the will of the people. Not that this always works in practice; most people would say that they have more important things to do than keeping an eye on their elected officials. Still, Japanese media offers ample access to Diet details, a net plus for citizens and residents.

The Diet contains two houses: the somewhat complicated "lower" House of Representatives, and the more straightforward "upper" House of Councillors. Akin to senators in the United States Congress, councillors are elected for six-year terms, with half up for renewal every three years. Representatives, by contrast, serve four-year terms—maybe. The thing is, the representatives can be kicked out ("dissolved") at any time by the prime minister, triggering a new election. (The House of Councillors cannot be dissolved, but simply pauses during this transition.)

Why would prime ministers do this? To get what they want. If things aren't going according to plan in the Diet, perhaps a fresh election will bring in a new crop of reps who are more aligned with Cabinet policies. This happens a lot; the average lower house endures only three years, and when the thirty-third House of Representatives ended its full term in December 1976, it took more than four decades for Japan to experience another undissolved house.

This wipe-out power works both ways; the Diet can call for a vote of "No Confidence" against the Cabinet, which, if successful, triggers resignation of all Cabinet ministers. But before resigning, the prime minister has ten days to turn right around and dissolve the House of Representatives that just tried to fire him. It's never a dull moment in Japanese politics.

When it manages to remain in session, how does the Diet exercise its organ of state power? Its primary duty is to deliberate and vote on legislation, a process I'll describe below. Here are some other ways it carries out the will of the people.

- Designate the new prime minister for a subsequent appointment by the emperor. This is the mandatory first task of any new PM-less Diet. If the two houses can't agree on a pick, the House of Representatives has the final say.

- Debate and approve a budget, a task that starts in the House of Representatives.
- Conduct investigations "in relation to government."
- Act as a court of impeachment for judges when needed.
- Approve treaties with other countries and international bodies.
- Set deliberation and discipline rules on a per-house basis.
- Select a president who can break ties in voting, and choose officers, all on a per-house basis.
- Keep and publish a record of its proceedings.
- Take responsibility for the Cabinet.
- Authorize gifts to and from the Imperial Household, including property.

The Diet has one ordinary session each year, currently scheduled for January and which runs 150 days. Emergency sessions can also be invoked by the Cabinet whenever there is, well, an emergency. With a few exceptions, legislative proceedings are open to the public. If the snippets on the TV news are any indication, these sessions can get feisty.

The Cabinet

In Japan's parliamentary system, the state's executive power is wielded by the Cabinet, consisting of a prime minister and other ministers of state. The Diet chooses a prime minister from its own ranks who in turn appoints the other ministers, at least half of whom must be active Diet members. What this means is that in Japan, the Cabinet and its executive functions are an extension of the legislature. The various bureaucratic agencies under Cabinet authority work without much legislative interference, although ministers over those departments can be called in front of the Diet for questioning. But as the Cabinet itself is made up mostly of active Diet members, the influence of the legislature on ministers cannot be ignored. Article 66 of the Constitution makes it even clearer: "The Cabinet, in the exercise of executive power, shall be collectively responsible to the Diet." This is surprising given that Americans within the post-war agency overseeing Japan's transition (GHQ) fleshed out much of the constitutional structure, and America itself has a strong separation between the executive and legislative branches.

The various state ministers may all seem like equals, but the prime minister is the chief over all others, and he can kick other ministers out any time he wants, lest they forget. Whenever a new prime minister comes into power, the previous Cabinet must resign *en masse*, allowing the new chief to set the tone and policy direction for the executive branch. Here is another fun fact about the Cabinet: Due to a bit of trouble with the Japanese government in the first half of the twentieth century, all Cabinet ministers must be civilians.

The Cabinet's primary role is to carry out its executive functions of enforcing Japan's laws, supervising the various administrative departments, and conducting foreign and domestic affairs of state. To accomplish this, the executive has an enormous bureaucratic apparatus, the modern counterpart to the centuries-old hierarchy of national and regional administrative offices. The ministers of state each oversee specific agencies, and from all appearances, the prime minister assigns these leadership roles based on an ability to advance policy goals and not necessarily because of a minister's subject-matter expertise.

The Cabinet can have up to seventeen ministers of state. As of this writing, there are twelve permanent Cabinet-level ministries.

- Ministry of Internal Affairs and Communications
- Ministry of Justice
- Ministry of Foreign Affairs
- Ministry of Finance
- Ministry of Education, Culture, Sports, Science and Technology
- Ministry of Health, Labour and Welfare
- Ministry of Agriculture, Forestry and Fisheries
- Ministry of Economy, Trade and Industry
- Ministry of Land, Infrastructure and Transport

- Ministry of the Environment
- Ministry of Defense
- Cabinet Office

There is also something called the Cabinet Secretariat. It acts as a traffic coordinator for all other ministries and Cabinet functions, working in coordination with the Cabinet Office, which has a slightly different overview focus. The head of the Secretariat is the Chief Cabinet Secretary, a position sometimes viewed as second only to the prime minister.

In addition to these key ministerial offices, the Cabinet can establish *ad hoc* and second-tier agencies or committees that are responsible to the full Cabinet. For example, the Minister for Reconstruction oversees the Reconstruction Agency, established in 2012 to coordinate the recovery efforts in the wake of the March 11, 2011, Tōhoku earthquake and tsunami. Another late addition is the State Minister of Digital Agency, created in 2021 to upgrade public and private digital infrastructure throughout Japan.

Beyond its executive role, the Cabinet also interfaces with and advises the Diet. Part of that responsibility involves submitting an annual budget to the House of Representatives. The Cabinet can also submit bills to the Diet for consideration, and its ministers are empowered to speak in legislative sessions to promote Cabinet policies. The Cabinet is required to report regularly to the Diet on its activities, and at least once per year, "the Cabinet shall report to the Diet and the people on the state of national finances."

When the Diet passes a new law, the cabinet minister who oversees that law's particular implementation will sign the law. The prime minister must also countersign all laws. This is a mandatory task, as the PM does not possess any veto power. The Cabinet can issue "cabinet orders" that have the feel of real laws. But in practice such orders can only clarify existing legislation.

Clearly, the Cabinet has a lot to do, but you haven't seen the last of it. Because the emperor doesn't have governmental power, any state-related action he performs requires the "advice and approval" of the Cabinet. The prime minister and his ministerial entourage also select the chief judge of the Supreme Court to be announced and appointed by the emperor. Finally, the Cabinet interacts with the judicial branch by appointing lower-tier court judges and making decisions on amnesties, pardons, and other restorations of rights for those convicted of crimes.

The Supreme Court and Inferior Courts

Japan has a typical modern judicial system, complete with judges, courts of appeal, a Supreme Court, and those black robes that are the latest fashion for judges. Jurisprudence is based on the rule of law with an encouragement (though no requirement) to value legal precedent. If you find yourself in the dock, you'll have access to a decent collection of legal rights, including prohibitions against *ex post facto* prosecution, self-incrimination, and double jeopardy, and all defendants have the right to legal counsel, provided at state expense if needed.

One common element that is missing from Japanese courtrooms, though, is a pool of jurors. Japan used to have trial by jury, but it was abolished during World War II. Instead, criminal and civil cases are typically heard by a panel of judges. Something that is new (since 2009) is the "lay judge" system. It has overlaps with the jury system in that members of the public are chosen at random to participate in court cases. But this isn't jury duty; it's judge duty! Naturally, the typical lay judge is not going to have a ready grasp of legal nuances that professional judges have spent their lives trying to understand. Therefore, while these citizen-judges do get to ask questions and issue verdicts just like the real judges, some handholding is required. Any guilty verdict, for instance, must be issued by a majority of the panel, a number that includes at least one professional judge. (A common configuration is three professional judges and six lay judges.)

The Constitution defined the basics of the Supreme Court, but almost everything else within the judicial branch was codified later through a combination of legislative acts and rules established by the highest court. The resulting unified court system handles everything from small claims to criminal treason. There are no municipal courts that deal with local cases. Instead, all civil and criminal trials are managed by a national system with five tiers.

- The most entry-level court is the Summary Court, with more than 400 such courthouses nationwide. These locations handle the most basic civil or criminal trials. Appeals to the next level are possible, but for small-claims suits, there is a single hearing with no opportunity to advance. All cases at this level are heard by a single judge.

- Family Courts are similar to Summary Courts, but deal exclusively with family-focused cases, especially inheritance and divorce situations. This tier has about fifty courthouses scattered across the nation. Many cases heard in these courts are closed to the public due to their personal and sensitive nature.

- The entry point for major cases is the District Court, and bad guys will find around fifty convenient locations across Japan. Cases on appeal from the first two tiers also get heard at this level. Proceedings take place before one to three judges depending on severity, with lay judges added for specific categories of trials.

- There are eight national High Courts that deal exclusively with appeals from more inferior courts. Some of these locations have branch benches that handle specialized cases, such as intellectual property law. All trials on this tier are heard by panels of judges.

- At the very top is the Supreme Court, the "court of last resort" for appeals and for laws that are challenged on constitutional grounds. Typical appeals come before a Petty Bench, with three to five judges making the final ruling. For cases where constitutional interpretation is a concern, a Grand Bench calls on nine to fifteen judges to decide.

Except for small-claims cases, any verdict can be appealed up to two times. For Summary Court cases, subsequent appeals are heard at the District and High Courts. For cases that begin in Family or District Courts, the progression is first to a High Court and then to the Supreme Court.

Having a national court system keeps everything standardized and consistent, something essential to a functioning judicial system. The Constitution also explicitly prohibits any kind of trial outside of the judicial branch—this dismantled the pre-war "Administrative Court" system that handled internal government cases—and there is a strict no-meddling rule around judges. Once appointed, a judge cannot be removed by the Diet or Cabinet except through a formal impeachment process or by being "judicially declared mentally or physically incompetent to perform official duties." But even though the other branches' hands are tied, the people can still act. Once every ten years, the voting public casts ballots to retain or dismiss sitting judges, so if some ruling comes down that is too obnoxious for public tastes, the people can remove the offending magistrate.

National Government Branches: Assemble!

Now that we have the parts, let's see how they work together to pass legislation, a core function of government. New laws begin life as bills submitted to one of the two chambers of the Diet. Members of either house can submit a new bill to their own chamber. The Cabinet can also submit new bills for consideration. Given that the Diet is the key legislative body, you would think that the entire law-passing process, from initial bright idea to the final victorious vote count, would normally be managed solely by these elected representatives. But it turns out that most bills originate with the Cabinet, or with one of the bureaucratic agencies contained within the executive branch.

For these agency-initiated bills, the text is first reviewed by the Cabinet Legislation Bureau before consideration by the full Cabinet. Once approved, the prime minister hands these new bills to either half of the Diet, although anything that is budget-related must go directly to the House of Representatives.

Each house has a collection of permanent, standing committees and special, *ad hoc* committees that focus on specific policy concerns. There are committees for national security, agriculture, technology, foreign affairs, healthcare, nuclear power, labor and employment, tourism, and the list goes on. New bills are sent to the committee that most closely aligns with its core intent, although complex bills may first go to a plenary committee which decides where it goes next.

Committees discuss and debate the text of new bills, question government ministers about the purposes of the proposed law, and bring in experts to get a handle on complicated legislation. That all sounds like fun, but eventually the committee must give a final up or down vote. A bill can die in committee, but there are also "railroading" procedures that push such defeated bills to the next stage.

Next comes the Plenary Sitting, where the results of the committee process are reviewed before invoking a house-level debate and voting process. If a bill gets a positive vote from that initial house, an identical bill still needs to be debated and voted on by the other chamber. This full-agreement rule is the standard, but if the houses can't pass identical bills, the House of Representatives has additional powers that allow it to override the version from the House of Councillors.

Once passed by the Diet, the Cabinet must sign the law; there is no veto power. The law is first signed by the relevant cabinet minister, and then countersigned by the prime minister. Finally, the emperor announces and promulgates the new law. Congratulations! Now obey the law.

But wait! If there is any doubt as to whether the new law is valid under the Constitution, the Supreme Court has the power "to determine the constitutionality of any law, order, regulation or official act." If it says, "no go," it's no go.

Political Parties in a Parliamentary System

One is such a lonely number, and so we have political parties. Politicians hope that by binding together in common cause, they can better advocate for their policies and constituencies. According to the law that details the Diet's structure, it takes only two people to form a legitimate political party, though the most successful ones have dozens or hundreds of active members.

Legislative victory requires a majority vote, and having a named group of like-minded people is the quickest way to accomplish this. But how many like-minded people have you ever met in your life? Even the Liberal Democratic Party (LDP, or in Japanese, *jimintō*), the group that has dominated the Diet throughout the post-war era, finds itself often coming up short, vote-wise. In Japan's parliamentary system, just as individual Diet members can come together under a party name, two or more parties can form coalitions, thinking that in unity they can push through their favorite laws. Of course, politics makes for strange futon-fellows, and often the enemy of my enemy is my coalition partner.

As of 2023, there are just under a dozen parties with members holding elective office in the Diet. The six largest parties claim 95 percent of those seats, listed here by number of seats held.

- Liberal Democratic Party (*jiyū minshu-tō*, abbreviated as *jimintō*) is the largest party and has consistently held a plurality of legislative seats since its founding in the 1950s. It is a big-tent conservative party, with second-tier factions coming together for shared purposes.

- Constitutional Democratic Party of Japan (*rikken minshu-tō*, abbreviated as *minshutō*) is a centrist-to-liberal party and the largest competitor to the dominant LDP. Although it is a relatively new party, it formed through a reorganization of earlier left-leaning groups.

- Japan Innovation Party (*nihon ishin no kai*) is a right-wing group with libertarian and populist sentiments. It grew out of a regional Ōsaka-based party.

- Kōmeitō (loosely translated as the "Fairness Party") is the political arm of Soka Gakkai, a Buddhist religious movement of the thirteenth century Nichiren school. Despite holding socialist views, they formed a coalition government with the right-leaning LDP for many years.

- Japanese Communist Party (*nihon kyōsan-tō*, abbreviated as *kyōsantō*) is, as its name implies, Japan's home for communism. A tad moderate in its leftist views, the JCP rejects the communist principle of violent revolution, instead embracing a policy of pacifism. As such, it opposes Japan's military alliance with the United States. By some accounts, even its adherence to progressivism has waned, instead setting itself up as a catch-all "Oppose Everything Party," especially when dealing with LDP proposals.
- Democratic Party for the People (*kokumin minshu-tō*) is a centrist-to-right party. Its members are holdouts from the merger of a similarly named group that decided to merge with the larger Constitutional Democratic Party of Japan.

Whichever party or coalition holds the majority of seats is referred to as *yotō* ("ruling party") in news reports. The groups in the minority are collectively known as *yatō* ("opposition party").

Regional and Municipal Governance

The Japanese Constitution includes strong support for regional and municipal government. The entire eighth chapter of that document is dedicated to "Local Self-Government." Article 92, which opens that block, goes out of its way to identify "the principle of local autonomy." In Japan, the people are the sovereigns, and those portions of government that come closest to the people will, by design, most closely reflect their authority. This is a key reason why the elected national legislature wields so much power compared to the other branches. It is also why local governments are guaranteed a significant level of freedom.

The Local Autonomy Law, passed by the Diet in 1947, details the independent authority held by municipalities. While the national government can pass laws that impact smaller jurisdictions, it must do so in a generic, evenly distributed way. Any law that targets a specific jurisdiction must also get local approval by enfranchised residents. Local legislatures are the main vehicle for deliberating matters of community import, and so long as they don't pass anything unconstitutional, these bodies, in theory, have a lot of say over what happens within their borders.

Japan's forty-seven prefectures are subdivided into approximately 1,700 municipal governments. During Japan's post-war growth period, there were closer to 3,200 such jurisdictions, but this number was culled after the 1990s-era collapse of the economic bubble, a restructuring known as the Great Heisei Consolidation. (All these numbers pale in comparison to the 70,000-plus distinct towns that covered pre-Meiji Japan.) Small communities wracked with debt were gobbled up by larger nearby cities better able to absorb such burdens. The shifting of young workers from rural communities to major cities, when combined with the early pangs of population decline across the nation, also reduced the need for so many legal enclaves.

Despite the ability for unbridled independence, there is a lot of uniformity across municipal bodies, thanks in part to administrative practices going back centuries. While city halls do manage processes specific to the local community, they also act as a local office for national bureaucratic services. That is due to so many government services— retirement accounts, health insurance, "My Number" card management, and so on—having been established at the national level. This offers a lot of conformity with procedures nationwide, but it can also take a bite out of municipal independence. Even with the self-autonomy principle in effect, prefectural and municipal governments in Japan display a lot less self-governance than, say, states and counties in the United States or cantons in Switzerland.

There is another tier of administration below the city level: the neighborhood association, known as *chōnaikai* or *jichikai* in Japanese. While these community-level groups don't have the same official standing as municipal governments, they traditionally have behaved like branches of the local government. In locations that have such groups, every home is automatically a member. Neighborhood groups collect membership fees, hold elections for leadership positions, and offer local support services, including disaster prevention, garbage collection, calisthenics programs (*rajio taisō*), sponsorship of local festivals, and programs for youth and seniors. Some associations even own their own property and host regular classes for community members.

Although they were abolished for a time after World War II, neighborhood associations returned in 1952 and became an important part of community life. In 1991, the Local Autonomy Law was revised to strengthen the legal status of these area groups. However, changes in population dynamics and in the priorities of households have worked to blunt the impact of these local associations. In some areas, less than half of all households bother to sign up at all, and there are neighborhoods where these groups have ceased to operate. While key functions will likely shift to city hall, the disappearance of these groups may have a significant impact on Japan's ability to quickly respond to emergencies in each region.

Legal Code and Regulations

Japan's legal system includes a hierarchy of documents and humans that carry the force of law. At the very top are the sovereign people of Japan—the humans I mentioned. Just below the people is the Constitution (*kempō*), which we met in Chapter 2. This is the highest law of the land, and all other laws or orders must adhere to its dictates. When the Supreme Court's Grand Bench rules on the validity of a law, it does so by holding it up to the light of the Constitution.

Those laws come primarily from the Diet, which votes and passes legislative acts during its ordinary and extraordinary sessions. Whereas the Constitution is terse and non-specific, laws passed by Japan's bicameral legislature can be linguistically dense, sometimes to the point of misunderstanding, which is why a court system is there to adjudicate conflicts with the law. Acts, once signed by the relevant cabinet ministers, are promulgated by the emperor, and published in the government's *Official Gazette*. This documentation is revised daily by the National Printing Bureau and available to the public for its immediate perusal and subsequent obedience.

Next come cabinet and ministerial orders (*seirei* and *meirei*). These law-like missives are issued by the Cabinet at large or individual ministries within the executive branch. Most often, they seek to clarify existing law, giving specific direction to bureaucratic agencies as to how particular aspects of the law should be implemented and enforced. These orders are legally binding, but the Diet is empowered to nullify such directives. The court as well can issue a halt to any order that is repugnant to the constitutional text.

Local ordinances (*jōrei*) include laws passed by prefectural and municipal jurisdictions. While they only impact residents in that geographic area, they have the same authority as laws passed by the national Diet, assuming there is no outright legal conflict. At the other end of the spectrum are treaties (*jōyaku*), law-like agreements with other countries, the United Nations, or other international bodies. Any treaty concluded by the Cabinet must receive approval from the Diet before it becomes binding on Japan. As with laws, there is an imperial promulgation process for these international contracts.

Finally, the three branches of government define and implement their own administrative procedures. Some of these are guides that streamline everyday tasks. Other procedures are more law-like, including the rules that the Supreme Court issues to direct the practices within the inferior courts. A step below laws, these administrative dictates can be altered or removed through actual laws or judicial review.

Security and International Policies

Japan went through an extreme isolationist phase during the Tokugawa shogunate, but like a kid who zooms out to the play field when the recess bell rings, it wasted no time in becoming one of the world's most connected nations once it eliminated the closed policy of *sakoku*. It now plays in the same sandbox with other advanced nations. Japan is a member of the G7 (Group of Seven), the G20 (Group of Twenty), and the QUAD (a security-focused dialog with Australia, India, and the United States). While it is not a permanent member of the United Nations Security Council, it has advocated for a reconstituted council where it sits in perpetuity with other so-called "G4 Nations" (Brazil, Germany, and India).

These cross-national relationships are defined through treaties, international agreements that you might think have teeth, but are sometimes implemented according to the whims of each member country. Yet such documents are considered law in Japan, and the Constitution insists that "treaties concluded by Japan...shall be faithfully observed." The negotiation of treaties is concluded by the Cabinet for subsequent approval by the Diet. Although a poorly crafted treaty could have dire consequences for the nation, they are much easier to bring into being than constitutional amendments, despite having the full force of law.

Each year, Japan announces its official position on all manner of international affairs through its *Diplomatic Bluebook*, published every spring (in Japanese) by the Ministry of Foreign Affairs. (A translation in English comes out at the end of each calendar year.) Weighing in at nearly 400 pages, the tome explains Japan's take on the world, sometimes with blunt clarity, but more often in the nuanced language of diplomats.

Shrine and State

As I mentioned back in the history chapter, the Shinto religious system played a significant role in state affairs leading up to World War II. The emperor was treated as a demigod, a direct descendant of the sun goddess, and therefore the administrative systems that governed in his name and under his sovereign authority were linked with religious expectations. Denigrating the Emperor was not simply an offense of *lèse-majesté*, it was a violation of right doctrine. This imperial worldview had a chilling effect on the normal course of political debate, allowing the nation's leaders to make unopposed decisions that, as it turned out, were not in Japan's long-term best interests.

To ensure such conflicts of interest would not occur going forward, the post-war governmental redesign managed by the Supreme Commander for the Allied Powers (GHQ) added constitutional language enforcing a separation between church and state. Article 20 requires that, "No religious organization shall receive any privileges from the State, nor exercise any political authority." The transition of the emperor from deity to governmental symbol helped this constitutional imperative become a practical reality. Still, there are groups, including a few news organizations of record, who yearn for a return to those days of yore, when men were men and emperors were gods.

While State Shinto is no longer legal, politicians still do religious things. Religious patterns permeate the enthronement rites for each new emperor, and Japan's Imperial Regalia—the sword, mirror, and jewel that are trotted out with each imperial change—are, I expect, still viewed by the Imperial Household as having been owned by

Amaterasu herself. Ministers of state continue to visit Yasukuni Shrine, a religious memorial for war veterans, conduct that always gets a strong reaction from Japan's neighbors.

Some politicians are on record opposing even these vestiges of the once-strong church-state system. Yet Japan's Supreme Court has regularly given its assent to such traditions. And politicians are allowed the same freedom of religious practice and freedom of assembly guaranteed to all other Japanese citizens. But it's not easy. The assassination of former Prime Minister Abe Shinzō was triggered by the cozy relationship that politicians had with the Unification Church, a quasi-Christian cult that emerged out of Korea.

Despite the shocking nature of that murder, freedom of religion is still the standard in Japan. Modern Japan is pluralistic in its religious temperament, and it is commonly accepted that Japanese are "born Shinto, married Christian, buried Buddhist." The government has adapted to this reality, withdrawing the overtly religious textbooks that were the standard before the war, and in general taking a hands-off approach to the personal spiritual practices of its residents.

Voting and Popular Sovereignty

Article 15 of Japan's Constitution guarantees that "the people have the inalienable right to choose their public officials and to dismiss them." These officers, who are "servants of the whole community," are chosen through non-compulsory secret ballots cast by enfranchised Japanese adults. It wasn't always this way. Democracy as we know it today did not exist in Japan for most of its history, and the *demos* had few, if any, rights to select leaders during the country's feudal era. Instead, officials earned their positions through patronage, oligarchy, heredity, or outright military conquest.

Enter the Enlightenment and its romance with democracy and popular sovereignty. The new Meiji Constitution, at least on paper, granted the people a level of authority in selecting government leaders. It stipulated a national system of elections to be defined in law, and its initial form granted the franchise to taxpaying, male property owners, a limited pool initially consisting of around 1 percent of the general population. This was extended to include all adult males in 1925, although they still did not have the loudest political voice. The House of Peers, a body of aristocrats, made up half of the Diet proper, and even if the voters got their favorites into office, the sovereign emperor could find a way to override any policy.

These days, with universal suffrage granted to all adults, just over half of eligible voters participate in even the most well-advertised elections, down from a post-war peak of almost 80 percent in the late 1950s. A 2016 adjustment to voting laws extended the franchise to eighteen- and nineteen-year-olds, hoping to open the societal discussion table to younger participants. As has been the case in other countries, young people tend not to vote.

If these youngsters were to cast ballots, they would do so once every three years for the House of Councillors, and once every four years for most other officials at the national, prefectural, and municipal levels. A system of Unified Local Elections tries to line up the election dates for all those with four-year terms regardless of jurisdiction, but some locations still have their own non-standard voting schedules. Then there's the prime minister's ability to wave his hand and dismiss the entire House of Representatives at will. Once dissolved, a fresh election for its seats must be held within forty days, which means the voters might be called upon to select new leaders at any moment.

Despite this wide variety in voting dates, the method of carrying out elections is highly regulated and uniform across the country. Candidates must attain a certain age to run for office, based on the assumption that age and wisdom go together. For prefectural governors and the House of Councillors, the minimum age is thirty. For all other offices (House of Representatives, prefectural legislatures, mayoral races), a mere twenty-five years is sufficient. As for the voters, eighteen is the minimum age for casting a ballot.

An election cycle begins with campaigns, opportunities for candidates to get the word out. In my own American homeland, campaigns can go on for years, especially at the national level. But in Japan, the timeline is highly condensed, and the smaller your constituency, the shorter the time allowed. Those running for the House of Councillors are allotted the most time, a full seventeen days to tell the public how wonderful their policies are. At the short end of the stick are mayoral races for towns under 50,000 residents. These poor hopefuls only get one week max to spread the political good news. The means of electioneering is also regulated, with rules that establish strict standards for campaign posters, television and radio broadcasts, and public speeches. If it weren't for the cars that drive around town blaring campaign messages from rooftop megaphones, you might not even notice that an election was happening. In fact, in some districts, electioneering doesn't need to happen at all. An expanding paucity of candidates in some remote districts means that many officials run uncontested. The number of these "walkover" seats has been growing, with more than a third of all electoral districts experiencing at least one such easy win.

Now we get to the hard part: the election. At the local level, voting is straightforward: the candidates with the most votes win. For offices with just a single winner—governor, mayor, and single-seat legislative districts—the elections department simply sorts all candidates by vote count and puts a "You're a Winner!" sticker next to the name on top.

For cities that have multi-seat constituencies, they will need a lot more stickers, but the math is the same. In these "first past the post" contests, victory goes to as many candidates from the top of the list as there are available seats. One outcome of this system is that you get a lot more party variety than you do in national politics. At the city level, personal charisma can propel a candidate across the line regardless of party affiliation. This is especially true when each voter is allowed to cast a ballot for multiple candidates. Once voters have added their personal favorite from their own party, they might add that interesting candidate from that bizzarro party that would never win in the Diet.

Compared to the simple math employed in local elections, Diet contests are complex affairs that attempt to balance the interests of the various voter constituencies and political parties by applying two parallel voting systems to each house. In the lower House of Representatives with its 460-ish members—seat counts are adjusted from time to time based on population and district allocation—about 60 percent are "single-seat constituencies," each decided by a plurality of voters.

The remainder use a "proportional representation" system, with all seats distributed among eleven geographic blocks. Voters cast two ballots, one for an individual candidate trying to obtain the single-seat office, and one for a political party who will share the seats allocated to the local geographic block. Those seats are given out to each party in proportion to how many votes those parties won from the second block-style ballot. It all sounds very complicated, and you should count your lucky stars that I'm not going to explain the intricate "d'Hondt method" calculations that are used to ensure a fair distribution to each party.

The upper House of Councillors also uses two parallel voting systems, but of course they don't align with the lower house's process. Councillors do run for single-seat constituencies, but some electoral districts have space for multiple winners. On the proportional half of the ballot, the seats distributed to political parties come from one large nationwide district instead of the eleven distinct blocks used by the lower house.

Citizenship

By now it should be clear that the government of Japan exists by the sovereign authority of its people. If you are like me, you are likely thinking, "I am just an ordinary person, but I really want to be a sovereign authority. Is that possible?" It absolutely is! In Japan, this authority flows from those individuals who are identified as citizens. Citizenship is acquired by birthright or through a naturalization process.

Birthright citizenship is by far the easier of the two, and if you are given a choice, I highly recommend going that route if only to cut down on the paperwork. The only requirement is that at least one of your parents be a Japanese citizen at the moment of your birth. (If the father was Japanese, but died prior to the birth, that also qualifies.) Your parents will need to register your birth with the government, but you personally don't need to do anything except drink milk and cry when your diaper becomes uncomfortable.

Parentage is the key here. Being born on Japanese soil to non-Japanese parents doesn't count. Well, that's the case most of the time. If you are born in Japan to stateless parents, or neither parent can be identified—is that even possible?—you can qualify as Japanese, but this path brings other problems, so it's best to stick with bona fide Japanese parents.

Sometimes a child will acquire two or more citizenships at birth from the parents. However, this multinational identification is fleeting. Once the child reaches the age of twenty-two, a decision to renounce one passport must be made, as Japan does not permit adults to hold multiple, simultaneous citizenships.

If you didn't acquire Japanese citizenship at birth—perhaps your parents were busy being citizens of another country that day—there is still the naturalization option. This path is available for those who have been residents of Japan for at least five years (or three years for spouses of Japanese citizens), and who opt to renounce any other national loyalties. While many naturalized citizens first acquired permanent residency, this is not a specific requirement for naturalization. Japanese language proficiency is also not mandatory, although financial self-sufficiency (or reliance on a self-sufficient family member) must be demonstrated before citizenship is granted.

If the Japanese government approves your application for citizenship—congratulations! You are the sovereign people! Of course, this doesn't mean you can do whatever you want—see the previous chapters that discuss the rights and duties of citizenship. But naturalized citizens are entitled to all the same rights offered to those with birthright citizenship, including the voting franchise, the ability to run for elected office, and the freedom to complain about those who run for elected office.

CHAPTER FIVE

Japan's Economy

In the previous chapter, I briefly mentioned how the Diet initiates legislation on budget issues. This all assumes that there is money in the treasury to be budgeted. In this final chapter, we will examine where the Japanese government gets this money and how it chooses to spend it.

Before we get into Japan's specific situation, now would be a good time to remind you that governments don't make any money. Well, that's not completely true. Governments *print* money, and printing is a form of making. But those paper and metal tokens are stand-ins for the true resources provided by others, a portion of which gets sent to government coffers each year. A nation's citizens typically generate the lion's share of these "contributions" through the payment of taxes. Countries also derive revenue from external sources, including import duties paid by foreign entities who wish to sell their wares in-country. Regardless of the source, government expenditures are a method of obtaining funds from individuals and groups only to turn right around and give those same funds to another set of individuals and groups.

Not that any of this is inherently immoral. In democratic systems where sovereignty rests with the people, the citizens have decided to entrust the government with various collective duties, and those duties cost a lot of money. Paying taxes is no fun, but as botanists have repeatedly failed in their mandate to grow real money trees, the responsibility to pay for these services falls on the population that demanded them in the first place. Seen in this way, government budgets are simply a joint budget for members of society, where a portion of each resident's income is designated for retirement programs, self-defense systems, road construction, primary and secondary schools, bureaucratic salaries, and welfare programs. There happens to be a line item in that budget called "your own money," the amount left over after you have paid all your taxes and government fees. Citizens have the right to adjust the master budget through their representatives. But once published, those same citizens agree to fund each line item from their own pockets.

Whether you are a fiscal conservative who believes the government's belt can always be tightened a bit more, or a bleeding-heart progressive who welcomes any opportunity to redistribute a nation's largess, the funds still ultimately come from you. For this reason alone, residents need to be aware of the economic systems that are handling a significant portion of their incomes. So, let's get to it.

Government Revenues

While you are the source of most government revenues, tax officers rarely show up at your door and say, "That will be one million yen, please." Instead, the government establishes a variety of inscrutable programs to collect the necessary funds from you and your neighbors. Taxes are collected at the national, prefectural, and municipal levels, a complex mishmash of mandatory payments that might raise your blood pressure were I to list them all out.

Fortunately, the Ministry of Finance provides a high-level summary that covers all levels of taxation. These revenue sources fall into three broad categories. The percentages shown here come from the government's tax breakdown for 2023 (see Figure 5-1, although that chart mixes in non-tax revenue sources).[1]

1. **Income Taxes.** Japan receives most of its funds from this source, around 51.8 percent of the entire budget. Three-fifths of this amount comes directly from individuals through personal income taxes (managed by the National Tax Agency) and residency taxes (managed jointly by prefectural and municipal governments). The remaining two-fifths of this source is acquired through corporate income taxes. After the 2011 Tōhoku tsunami disaster, a special "reconstruction tax" was added to this

---

1 Visit www.mof.go.jp/tax_policy/summary/condition/a01.htm to read up on the specifics (in Japanese).

category. It is scheduled to sunset in 2037. But sometimes plans change, so that big-screen TV you were hoping to buy in 2038 might need to wait.

2. **Property Taxes.** These are annual or one-time charges on property that is held or transferred, and they provide about 13.3 percent of Japan's governmental revenues. Nearly two-thirds of such taxes come from the sale and subsequent annual assessment of real property—think houses, office buildings, and condominiums. The next biggest chunk, about a sixth of all property taxes, comes from inheritance and gift taxes. Fees for government services also appear in this category, including the stamps you affix to various government forms at city hall.

3. **Consumption Taxes.** This is the fee that hits you every time you pay for any good or service, or fill up your gas tank, or take a swig of booze, or take a swing at a golf ball. If a product or activity can be taxed, it is happening here, bringing in the remaining 34.8 percent of all government revenues. Seventy percent of this comes through the formal Consumption Tax, a percent-based levy that impacts most goods and services. In 2019, the government lifted this consumption tax from 8 percent to 10 percent, and it is already thinking about rates of 15

percent or more from a 1989 starting point of just 3 percent. Import duties get thrown into this bucket, as do power-generation taxes, tobacco taxes, hunting-license taxes, airline-fuel taxes, and—wouldn't you know it—public-bath taxes.

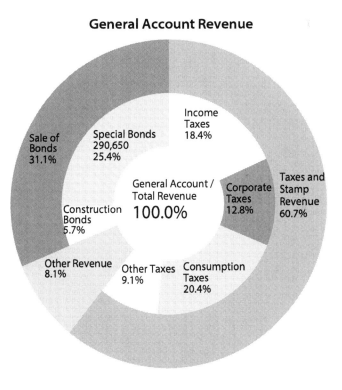

General Account Revenue

Figure 5-1. Distribution of government revenue (2023 budget).

With so much taxing to do, you would think that the government would need to get ordinary people to do most of that tax collecting—and it does. Every time you buy a piece of sushi at a restaurant or upgrade your old kimono for this year's model, the shopkeeper is acting as an arm of the government, collecting a little bit of tax from you with every purchase and forwarding those amounts to the local or national treasury.

But you needn't go all the way into town to pony up some tax money. You can pay taxes right from the comfort and safety of your home by filling out your annual income tax forms. Japan has a highly progressive income tax system, with rates that start at 5 percent for those with little income, zooming up to 45 percent for income that exceeds forty million yen per year (2023 numbers). Don't forget to add the 2.1 percent Tōhoku reconstruction tax. But wait! You also pay an additional 10 percent for your residency taxes, an amount that is shared between your prefecture and your local municipality. And so far, I have only discussed the portion paid by individuals. Businesses also pay taxes, which of course they pass on to consumers through the prices of their products.

For households making under twenty million yen per year from a single job, the income tax paperwork is often handled by the employer. The company withholds tax from each paycheck, adjusting as needed throughout the year to account for standard deductions and changes in income. Assuming the calculations are right, the company submits those taxes and accompanying paperwork in the name of the taxpayer, freeing the employee from the burden of running the numbers manually.

This is bad. You only need to look back a handful of paragraphs to see that the national budget is really the people's budget. Hiding the details behind a veneer of convenience has the (possibly) unintended side effect of keeping taxpayers out of the loop when it comes to government spending. But I digress. Actually, I don't. The reason why all budget bills begin in the House of Representatives is because that is the part of government most closely aligned with the will of the voters in particular, and the citizenry in general. And the reason that the Constitution (in Article 91) demands that the Cabinet report financial information annually to the people is because it is important. Okay, end of diatribe.

Government Debt

I was going to wait until you were a bit older to tell you this, boys and girls, but sometimes your government spends more money than it has. To accomplish this seemingly impossible feat, it borrows money. Lots of money. For Japan in particular, more money than any other country on earth. And because you are old enough, I will tell you how this happened.

All governments go into debt for long-term, large-scale infrastructure projects, such as the construction of highway systems, government offices, shipping ports, and the like. To fund such projects, jurisdictions issue bonds, fixed-length IOUs that are paid back with a defined amount of interest. Lots of people buy bonds because of the guaranteed interest and the relative security as an investment.

Japan has a lot of infrastructure, so it issues a lot of bonds. Depending on the purpose of a bond, it might come to maturity anywhere between two and forty years from the time of purchase. When it comes time to pay the bonds back, its principal and interest must be paid for out of the jurisdiction's own funds, and ultimately by the taxpayer. For this reason, the public has been hesitant about issuing too many bonds or borrowing for seemingly useless projects.

If this was the extent of Japan's borrowing habits, it would be a lot like any other developed nation. But Japan uses bonds for another purpose that impacts its economic health: quantitative easing. Japan's economy used to be hot, really hot. And then in 1992, it wasn't. You can read up on the "asset price bubble" that caused the entire meltdown, but for our purposes, the key is that the Japanese government felt it needed to do something to fix the problems leftover from the collapse of the bubble.

In a quantitative easing scenario, the government still sells bonds, but then it buys most of them back using its own money, by which I mean using the taxpayers' money. But taxpayers don't pay right away. Instead, the Bank of Japan declares that more money is magically available on its balance sheet—national banks can do that—and uses that "free" money to buy public and corporate bonds from financial institutions, all in the hope that those institutions will loan out the monies paid to you and me and get the economy roaring again. No, I don't understand it either.

There is lot of debate about whether quantitative easing programs are any good. Japan has been running one since 2001 and the economy still has significant issues. There is also the problem of debt servicing, the need for the government to find money to pay off bonds as they become due. Yet another concern is that when the Bank of Japan "prints" more money through fiat declaration, it is devaluing the existing pool of money already moving around the economy.

In 2013, Prime Minister Abe instituted a series of economic reforms collectively known as "Abenomics," policies that included a sizable quantitative easing component. The results were again mixed at best. Since that attempt, the global pandemic, the continuing impact of the 2011 Tōhoku disaster, and the economic transition caused by Japan's declining population have dramatically increased the country's indebtedness to itself.

As of this writing, about one-third of the nation's annual revenue comes from the sale of government bonds to the Bank of Japan and the public at large, thrusting the cumulative debt ever higher. This is all so vexing, and it will need to be dealt with in the long term. But a key short-term benefit of all this borrowing is that it allows Japan and its various jurisdictions to fund current expenses as if they were paying with actual money. Let's consider that portion of the fiscal process.

Government Expenses

The items that make up the Japanese government's annual budget are akin to things you might find in a family budget: healthcare, funding of building repairs and other capital expenses, paying off loans, providing for the common defense, stuff like that.

Japan's fiscal year runs from April 1 to March 31, so approval of the budget for the upcoming year needs to be finalized in March. The budgeting process is months in the making and involves every unit of government.

- Between June and August, government agencies consider how much money they will need the following year. This includes not only those departments overseen by the executive branch, but also those funds needed by the Diet and Supreme Court to run their respective branches. These individual budget estimates are submitted to the Ministry of Finance.

- The Ministry of Finance works with each agency and cabinet ministers to adjust those draft estimates based on policy priorities and expected revenues. Once all adjustments are complete, the Cabinet approves the final budget.
- The Cabinet submits this budget to the House of Representatives in January. The constituencies engage in a battle of wits and spreadsheets over the details. Once each line item has been fine-tuned to the perfect financial amount, the representatives vote on and approve the full budget by early March.
- Debate moves into the House of Councillors, which must also give its assent. Any disagreements between the two chambers go through a reconciliation process. If the two houses still can't agree, the House of Representatives gets the final say. Passage by the full Diet occurs in mid- to late-March.
- The government starts spending your money on April 1.

Most of the focus is on the general budget, and when you complain that your taxes are too high, you are usually referring to some point of frustration in that budget. Japan also manages a dozen or so "special budgets," balance sheets that focus on a single government-funded project. Some of these are used to facilitate long-term payments, such as paying down the national debt. Others exist to oversee inter-jurisdictional exchanges, such as when the national government sends funds to regional governments. Insurance coverage and pension programs for workers also get their own special budgets.

Prefectures and municipalities go through a similar budget process each year, albeit with less yen to play with. In 2007, Japan instituted a series of tax-related changes known as the "Trinity Reforms," named for its three core policy changes. Throughout the post-war era, the population dynamics within Japan shifted from rural to urban areas, draining many prefectures of people and tax revenues. Under the new system, Japan sought to prop up struggling prefectures, bolster local autonomy, and further decentralize government functions, especially those that didn't require oversight from Tōkyō. The reforms also instituted the *furusato nōzei* system, which allows urban taxpayers to direct a percentage of their income taxes toward specific local jurisdictions in other prefectures. Participation in this scheme is enhanced by "return gifts" sent from the receiving community back to contributing taxpayers.

These tax transfers represent a significant portion of the overall national budget. But don't worry, there are plenty of other things that the government gets to pay for. Social security programs and servicing the national debt together consume more than half of all tax revenues. Other major spending areas include national defense, reconstruction from the 2011 disaster, public education, and capital expenditures. Figure 5-2 shows the expense categories for the 2023 budget.[1]

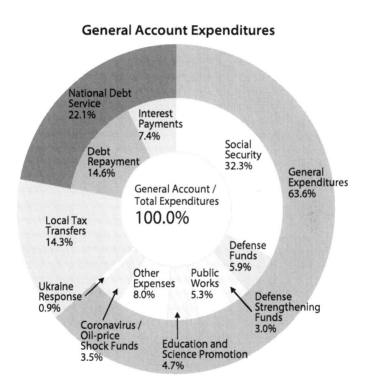

General Account Expenditures

Figure 5-2. Distribution of government expenses (2023 budget).

1 Access page 13 of www.mof.go.jp/policy/budget/budger_workflow/budget/fy2023/ seifuan2023/01.pdf to read up on the specifics (in Japanese).

Japan is at a difficult time in terms of its tax base. Already working to service one of the highest debt ratios in the world, the country must also contend with a decreasing number of taxpayers who need to support an expanding elder class and its greater healthcare needs. The coronavirus pandemic added to the surprise costs already incurred from the 2011 tsunami and nuclear disaster. Plus, international concerns carry a cost, as shown by the new Ukraine-related line item in the 2023 budget, not to mention a hefty increase in defense-related expenditures. The annual budgeting process attempts to meld all these demands into something palatable to the general public. Ultimately, that same public has the final say in what to pay for, their desires expressed through their elected representatives.

Board of Audit

The Japanese government's spending habits pass through a regular financial audit to keep things above board and accurate. Politicians and government agencies don't submit to this inspection out of the goodness of their hearts; they are required to do so by constitutional mandate. Article 90 of the modern Constitution makes it clear: "Final accounts of the expenditures and revenues of the State shall be audited annually by a Board of Audit."

That clause goes on to say that the "organization and competency" of the board is left up to legislators to decide, which seems like a "one step forward, two steps back" scenario. But it turns out that Japan's Board of Audit does a proper job, and by law is fully independent from the Cabinet and its money-spending ways. None of this prevents the government from overspending, but it does make such excesses a matter of validated public record.

The Board of Audit performs mandatory reviews all branches of the national government, plus some other agencies where more than half of the budget comes from the government. It also performs periodic "discretionary" audits on several hundred organizations—both fully private and public-private partnerships—that receive funding from the government or that serve a public function normally managed by governments. This includes universities, transportation agencies, the Bank of Japan, the national pension service, the organizations that run key airports, the Japan [Horse] Racing Association, and the public broadcaster NHK.

The published audits are made available to the public for review. You're probably already busy this afternoon, but if you have a chance, why not take a gander? The agency releases all audits in Japanese, but English translations eventually appear.

Fiscal Policy and the Bank of Japan

According to the Bank of Japan Act, the objective of the nation's central bank is "to issue banknotes and to carry out currency and monetary control," and "to ensure smooth settlement of funds among banks and other financial institutions, thereby contributing to the maintenance of stability of the financial system." It seems complicated, especially to someone like me who is still trying to remember who those people are that appear on Japan's currency.

As I mentioned at the start of this chapter, governments don't make money, but instead print money. The Bank of Japan performs this function, issuing coinage and script that helps individuals and businesses engage in economic activity. But its role goes far beyond these physical tokens of value, especially these days when so much economic activity occurs without anyone physically handling paper money.

The Bank of Japan performs these key functions within the economy.

- Issuing of banknotes, although somewhat philosophically as the actual printing of currency and minting of coins are performed by the National Printing Bureau and the Japan Mint, respectively.

- Providing settlement services at the highest level, a guarantee of charges that helps stabilize the broader economy.

- Defining Japan's monetary policy, primarily by setting the core interest rate, which further impacts the ability for financial institutions to lend funds to individuals and businesses.

- Acting as the national treasury for government deposits.

To better understand all this, I recommend getting a Ph.D. in economic theory, because anything less than that is going to leave you with too many lingering questions.

The Private Sector

Although the Bank of Japan controls the money supply in order to bring price stability to the national economy, ultimately the wealth of nations—thank you, Adam Smith—rests with the people. In the case of Japan, that's great news since this population also happens to be the sovereign authority for the country.

Some people believe that the rich are hoarding all the money, and those videos of influencers filling a swimming pool with dollar bills does nothing to dispel this narrative. But wealth is created in the simplest of acts. If you buy ¥1,000 worth of vegetables and spices (and overhead expenses), spend an hour or two making a tasty soup, and sell it to passersby for ¥1,500, you just added real value to the economy.

Life, of course, is more than soup, and the actual generation of value is complex and risky. This is a key reason why the Bank of Japan is added as a layer on top the people's economic activity. But it is the everyday economic enterprise of the private sector that makes the economy possible in the first place, and yet another indication that the true value of Japan rests in its people, including immigrants.

Text of the Constitution of Japan

Japan promulgated its current Constitution on November 3, 1946, with an effective date six months later, on March 3, 1947. It fully replaced the previous Meiji-era Constitution of 1889.

The Edict of Promulgation and Signatures

I rejoice that the foundation for the construction of a new Japan has been laid according to the will of the Japanese people, and hereby sanction and promulgate the amendments of the Imperial Japanese Constitution effected following the consultation with the Privy Council and the decision of the Imperial Diet made in accordance with Article 73 of the said Constitution.

(Imperial Seal of the Emperor)

This third day of the eleventh month of the twenty-first year of Shōwa (November 3, 1946)

Countersigned:

Prime Minister and concurrently Minister for Foreign Affairs Yoshida Shigeru

Minister of State Baron Shidehara Kijūrō

Minister of Justice Kimura Tokutarō

Minister for Home Affairs Ōmura Seiichi

Minister of Education Tanaka Kōtarō

Minister of Agriculture and Forestry Wada Hirō

Minister of State Saito Takao

Minister of Communications Hitotsumatsu Sadayoshi

Minister of Commerce and Industry Hoshijima Nirō

Minister of Welfare Kawai Yoshinari

Minister of State Uehara Etsujirō

Minister of Transportation Hiratsuka Tsunejirō

Minister of Finance Ishibashi Tanzan

Minister of State Kanamori Tokujirō

Minister of State Zen Keinosuke

The Preamble

We, the Japanese people, acting through our duly elected
representatives in the National Diet, determined that we
shall secure for ourselves and our posterity the fruits of
peaceful cooperation with all nations and the blessings of
liberty throughout this land, and resolved that never again
shall we be visited with the horrors of war through the
action of government, do proclaim that sovereign power
resides with the people and do firmly establish this
Constitution. Government is a sacred trust of the people,
the authority for which is derived from the people, the
powers of which are exercised by the representatives of the
people, and the benefits of which are enjoyed by the people.

This is a universal principle of mankind upon which this Constitution is founded. We reject and revoke all constitutions, laws, ordinances, and rescripts in conflict herewith.

We, the Japanese people, desire peace for all time and are deeply conscious of the high ideals controlling human relationship, and we have determined to preserve our security and existence, trusting in the justice and faith of the peace-loving peoples of the world. We desire to occupy an honored place in an international society striving for the preservation of peace, and the banishment of tyranny and slavery, oppression and intolerance for all time from the earth. We recognize that all peoples of the world have the right to live in peace, free from fear and want.

We believe that no nation is responsible to itself alone, but that laws of political morality are universal; and that obedience to such laws is incumbent upon all nations who would sustain their own sovereignty and justify their sovereign relationship with other nations.

We, the Japanese people, pledge our national honor to accomplish these high ideals and purposes with all our resources.

Chapter I: The Emperor

Article 1. The Emperor shall be the symbol of the State and of the unity of the People, deriving his position from the will of the people with whom resides sovereign power.

Article 2. The Imperial Throne shall be dynastic and succeeded to in accordance with the Imperial House Law passed by the Diet.

Article 3. The advice and approval of the Cabinet shall be required for all acts of the Emperor in matters of state, and the Cabinet shall be responsible therefor.

Article 4. The Emperor shall perform only such acts in matters of state as are provided for in this Constitution and he shall not have powers related to government.

The Emperor may delegate the performance of his acts in matters of state as may be provided by law.

Article 5. When, in accordance with the Imperial House Law, a Regency is established, the Regent shall perform his acts in matters of state in the Emperor's name. In this case, paragraph one of the preceding article will be applicable.

Article 6. The Emperor shall appoint the Prime Minister as designated by the Diet.

The Emperor shall appoint the Chief Judge of the Supreme Court as designated by the Cabinet.

Article 7. The Emperor, with the advice and approval of the Cabinet, shall perform the following acts in matters of state on behalf of the people:

- Promulgation of amendments of the constitution, laws, cabinet orders and treaties.
- Convocation of the Diet.
- Dissolution of the House of Representatives.

- Proclamation of general election of members of the Diet.
- Attestation of the appointment and dismissal of Ministers of State and other officials as provided for by law, and of full powers and credentials of Ambassadors and Ministers.
- Attestation of general and special amnesty, commutation of punishment, reprieve, and restoration of rights.
- Awarding of honors.
- Attestation of instruments of ratification and other diplomatic documents as provided for by law.
- Receiving foreign ambassadors and ministers.
- Performance of ceremonial functions.

Article 8. No property can be given to, or received by, the Imperial House, nor can any gifts be made therefrom, without the authorization of the Diet.

Chapter II: Renunciation of War

Article 9. Aspiring sincerely to an international peace based on justice and order, the Japanese people forever renounce war as a sovereign right of the nation and the threat or use of force as means of settling international disputes.

In order to accomplish the aim of the preceding paragraph, land, sea, and air forces, as well as other war potential, will never be maintained. The right of belligerency of the state will not be recognized.

Chapter III: Rights and Duties of the People

Article 10. The conditions necessary for being a Japanese national shall be determined by law.

Article 11. The people shall not be prevented from enjoying any of the fundamental human rights. These fundamental human rights guaranteed to the people by this Constitution shall be conferred upon the people of this and future generations as eternal and inviolate rights.

Article 12. The freedoms and rights guaranteed to the people by this Constitution shall be maintained by the constant endeavor of the people, who shall refrain from any abuse of these freedoms and rights and shall always be responsible for utilizing them for the public welfare.

Article 13. All of the people shall be respected as individuals. Their right to life, liberty, and the pursuit of happiness shall, to the extent that it does not interfere with the public welfare, be the supreme consideration in legislation and in other governmental affairs.

Article 14. All of the people are equal under the law and there shall be no discrimination in political, economic or social relations because of race, creed, sex, social status or family origin.

Peers and peerage shall not be recognized.

No privilege shall accompany any award of honor, decoration or any distinction, nor shall any such award be valid beyond the lifetime of the individual who now holds or hereafter may receive it.

Article 15. The people have the inalienable right to choose their public officials and to dismiss them.

All public officials are servants of the whole community and not of any group thereof.

Universal adult suffrage is guaranteed with regard to the election of public officials.

In all elections, secrecy of the ballot shall not be violated. A voter shall not be answerable, publicly or privately, for the choice he has made.

Article 16. Every person shall have the right of peaceful petition for the redress of damage, for the removal of public officials, for the enactment, repeal or amendment of laws, ordinances or regulations and for other matters; nor shall any person be in any way discriminated against for sponsoring such a petition.

Article 17. Every person may sue for redress as provided by law from the State or a public entity, in case he has suffered damage through illegal act of any public official.

Article 18. No person shall be held in bondage of any kind. Involuntary servitude, except as punishment for crime, is prohibited.

Article 19. Freedom of thought and conscience shall not be violated.

Article 20. Freedom of religion is guaranteed to all. No religious organization shall receive any privileges from the State, nor exercise any political authority.

No person shall be compelled to take part in any religious act, celebration, rite or practice.

The State and its organs shall refrain from religious education or any other religious activity.

Article 21. Freedom of assembly and association as well as speech, press and all other forms of expression are guaranteed.

No censorship shall be maintained, nor shall the secrecy of any means of communication be violated.

Article 22. Every person shall have freedom to choose and change his residence and to choose his occupation to the extent that it does not interfere with the public welfare.

Freedom of all persons to move to a foreign country and to divest themselves of their nationality shall be inviolate.

Article 23. Academic freedom is guaranteed.

Article 24. Marriage shall be based only on the mutual consent of both sexes and it shall be maintained through mutual cooperation with the equal rights of husband and wife as a basis.

With regard to choice of spouse, property rights, inheritance, choice of domicile, divorce and other matters pertaining to marriage and the family, laws shall be enacted from the standpoint of individual dignity and the essential equality of the sexes.

Article 25. All people shall have the right to maintain the minimum standards of wholesome and cultured living.

In all spheres of life, the State shall use its endeavors for the promotion and extension of social welfare and security, and of public health.

Article 26. All people shall have the right to receive an equal education correspondent to their ability, as provided by law.

All people shall be obligated to have all boys and girls under their protection receive ordinary education as provided for by law. Such compulsory education shall be free.

Article 27. All people shall have the right and the obligation to work.

Standards for wages, hours, rest and other working conditions shall be fixed by law.

Children shall not be exploited.

Article 28. The right of workers to organize and to bargain and act collectively is guaranteed.

Article 29. The right to own or to hold property is inviolable.

Property rights shall be defined by law, in conformity with the public welfare.

Private property may be taken for public use upon just compensation therefor.

Article 30. The people shall be liable to taxation as provided by law.

Article 31. No person shall be deprived of life or liberty, nor shall any other criminal penalty be imposed, except according to procedure established by law.

Article 32. No person shall be denied the right of access to the courts.

Article 33. No person shall be apprehended except upon warrant issued by a competent judicial officer which specifies the offense with which the person is charged, unless he is apprehended, the offense being committed.

Article 34. No person shall be arrested or detained without being at once informed of the charges against him or without the immediate privilege of counsel; nor shall he be detained without adequate cause; and upon demand of any person such cause must be immediately shown in open court in his presence and the presence of his counsel.

Article 35. The right of all persons to be secure in their homes, papers and effects against entries, searches and seizures shall not be impaired except upon warrant issued for adequate cause and particularly describing the place to be searched and things to be seized, or except as provided by Article 33.

Each search or seizure shall be made upon separate warrant issued by a competent judicial officer.

Article 36. The infliction of torture by any public officer and cruel punishments are absolutely forbidden.

Article 37. In all criminal cases the accused shall enjoy the right to a speedy and public trial by an impartial tribunal.

He shall be permitted full opportunity to examine all witnesses, and he shall have the right of compulsory process for obtaining witnesses on his behalf at public expense.

At all times the accused shall have the assistance of competent counsel who shall, if the accused is unable to secure the same by his own efforts, be assigned to his use by the State.

Article 38. No person shall be compelled to testify against himself.

Confession made under compulsion, torture or threat, or after prolonged arrest or detention shall not be admitted in evidence.

No person shall be convicted or punished in cases where the only proof against him is his own confession.

Article 39. No person shall be held criminally liable for an act which was lawful at the time it was committed, or of which he has been acquitted, nor shall he be placed in double jeopardy.

Article 40. Any person, in case he is acquitted after he has been arrested or detained, may sue the State for redress as provided by law.

Chapter IV: The Diet

Article 41. The Diet shall be the highest organ of state power, and shall be the sole law-making organ of the State.

Article 42. The Diet shall consist of two Houses, namely the House of Representatives and the House of Councillors.

Article 43. Both Houses shall consist of elected members, representative of all the people.

The number of the members of each House shall be fixed by law.

Article 44. The qualifications of members of both Houses and their electors shall be fixed by law. However, there shall be no discrimination because of race, creed, sex, social status, family origin, education, property or income.

Article 45. The term of office of members of the House of Representatives shall be four years. However, the term shall be terminated before the full term is up in case the House of Representatives is dissolved.

Article 46. The term of office of members of the House of Councillors shall be six years, and election for half the members shall take place every three years.

Article 47. Electoral districts, method of voting and other matters pertaining to the method of election of members of both Houses shall be fixed by law.

Article 48. No person shall be permitted to be a member of both Houses simultaneously.

Article 49. Members of both Houses shall receive appropriate annual payment from the national treasury in accordance with law.

Article 50. Except in cases provided by law, members of both Houses shall be exempt from apprehension while the Diet is in session, and any members apprehended before the opening of the session shall be freed during the term of the session upon demand of the House.

Article 51. Members of both Houses shall not be held liable outside the House for speeches, debates or votes cast inside the House.

Article 52. An ordinary session of the Diet shall be convoked once per year.

Article 53. The Cabinet may determine to convoke extraordinary sessions of the Diet. When a quarter or more of the total members of either House makes the demand, the Cabinet must determine on such convocation.

Article 54. When the House of Representatives is dissolved, there must be a general election of members of the House of Representatives within forty (40) days from the date of dissolution, and the Diet must be convoked within thirty (30) days from the date of the election.

When the House of Representatives is dissolved, the House of Councillors is closed at the same time. However, the Cabinet may in time of national emergency convoke the House of Councillors in emergency session.

Measures taken at such session as mentioned in the proviso of the preceding paragraph shall be provisional and shall become null and void unless agreed to by the House of Representatives within a period of ten (10) days after the opening of the next session of the Diet.

Article 55. Each House shall judge disputes related to qualifications of its members. However, in order to deny a seat to any member, it is necessary to pass a resolution by a majority of two-thirds or more of the members present.

Article 56. Business cannot be transacted in either House unless one-third or more of total membership is present.

All matters shall be decided, in each House, by a majority of those present, except as elsewhere provided in the Constitution, and in case of a tie, the presiding officer shall decide the issue.

Article 57. Deliberation in each House shall be public. However, a secret meeting may be held where a majority of two-thirds or more of those members present passes a resolution therefor.

Each House shall keep a record of proceedings. This record shall be published and given general circulation, excepting such parts of proceedings of secret session as may be deemed to require secrecy.

Upon demand of one-fifth or more of the members present, votes of the members on any matter shall be recorded in the minutes.

Article 58. Each House shall select its own president and other officials.

Each House shall establish its rules pertaining to meetings, proceedings and internal discipline, and may punish members for disorderly conduct. However, in order to expel a member, a majority of two-thirds or more of those members present must pass a resolution thereon.

Article 59. A bill becomes a law on passage by both Houses, except as otherwise provided by the Constitution.

A bill which is passed by the House of Representatives, and upon which the House of Councillors makes a decision different from that of the House of Representatives, becomes a law when passed a second time by the House of Representatives by a majority of two-thirds or more of the members present.

The provision of the preceding paragraph does not preclude the House of Representatives from calling for the meeting of a joint committee of both Houses, provided for by law.

Failure by the House of Councillors to take final action within sixty (60) days after receipt of a bill passed by the House of Representatives, time in recess excepted, may be determined by the House of Representatives to constitute a rejection of the said bill by the House of Councillors.

Article 60. The budget must first be submitted to the House of Representatives.

Upon consideration of the budget, when the House of Councillors makes a decision different from that of the House of Representatives, and when no agreement can be reached even through a joint committee of both Houses, provided for by law, or in the case of failure by the House of Councillors to take final action within thirty (30) days, the period of recess excluded, after the receipt of the budget passed by the House of Representatives, the decision of the House of Representatives shall be the decision of the Diet.

Article 61. The second paragraph of the preceding article applies also to the Diet approval required for the conclusion of treaties.

Article 62. Each House may conduct investigations in relation to government, and may demand the presence and testimony of witnesses, and the production of records.

Article 63. The Prime Minister and other Ministers of State may, at any time, appear in either House for the purpose of speaking on bills, regardless of whether they are members of the House or not. They must appear when their presence is required in order to give answers or explanations.

Article 64. The Diet shall set up an impeachment court from among the members of both Houses for the purpose of trying those judges against whom removal proceedings have been instituted.

Matters relating to impeachment shall be provided by law.

Chapter V: The Cabinet

Article 65. Executive power shall be vested in the Cabinet.

Article 66. The Cabinet shall consist of the Prime Minister, who shall be its head, and other Ministers of State, as provided for by law.

The Prime Minister and other Ministers of State must be civilians.

The Cabinet, in the exercise of executive power, shall be collectively responsible to the Diet.

Article 67. The Prime Minister shall be designated from among the members of the Diet by a resolution of the Diet. This designation shall precede all other business.

If the House of Representatives and the House of Councillors disagree and if no agreement can be reached even through a joint committee of both Houses, provided for by law, or the House of Councillors fails to make designation within ten (10) days, exclusive of the period of recess, after the House of Representatives has made designation, the decision of the House of Representatives shall be the decision of the Diet.

Article 68. The Prime Minister shall appoint the Ministers of State. However, a majority of their number must be chosen from among the members of the Diet.

The Prime Minister may remove the Ministers of State as he chooses.

Article 69. If the House of Representatives passes a non-confidence resolution, or rejects a confidence resolution, the Cabinet shall resign en masse, unless the House of Representatives is dissolved within ten (10) days.

Article 70. When there is a vacancy in the post of Prime Minister, or upon the first convocation of the Diet after a general election of members of the House of Representatives, the Cabinet shall resign en masse.

Article 71. In the cases mentioned in the two preceding articles, the Cabinet shall continue its functions until the time when a new Prime Minister is appointed.

Article 72. The Prime Minister, representing the Cabinet, submits bills, reports on general national affairs and foreign relations to the Diet and exercises control and supervision over various administrative branches.

Article 73. The Cabinet, in addition to other general administrative functions, shall perform the following functions:

- Administer the law faithfully; conduct affairs of state.
- Manage foreign affairs.

- Conclude treaties. However, it shall obtain prior or, depending on circumstances, subsequent approval of the Diet.
- Administer the civil service, in accordance with standards established by law.
- Prepare the budget, and present it to the Diet.
- Enact cabinet orders in order to execute the provisions of this Constitution and of the law. However, it cannot include penal provisions in such cabinet orders unless authorized by such law.
- Decide on general amnesty, special amnesty, commutation of punishment, reprieve, and restoration of rights.

Article 74. All laws and cabinet orders shall be signed by the competent Minister of State and countersigned by the Prime Minister.

Article 75. The Ministers of State, during their tenure of office, shall not be subject to legal action without the consent of the Prime Minister. However, the right to take that action is not impaired hereby.

Chapter VI: The Judiciary

Article 76. The whole judicial power is vested in a Supreme Court and in such inferior courts as are established by law.

No extraordinary tribunal shall be established, nor shall any organ or agency of the Executive be given final judicial power.

All judges shall be independent in the exercise of their conscience and shall be bound only by this Constitution and the laws.

Article 77. The Supreme Court is vested with the rule-making power under which it determines the rules of procedure and of practice, and of matters relating to attorneys, the internal discipline of the courts and the administration of judicial affairs.

Public procurators shall be subject to the rule-making power of the Supreme Court.

The Supreme Court may delegate the power to make rules for inferior courts to such courts.

Article 78. Judges shall not be removed except by public impeachment unless judicially declared mentally or physically incompetent to perform official duties. No disciplinary action against judges shall be administered by any executive organ or agency.

Article 79. The Supreme Court shall consist of a Chief Judge and such number of judges as may be determined by law; all such judges excepting the Chief Judge shall be appointed by the Cabinet.

The appointment of the judges of the Supreme Court shall be reviewed by the people at the first general election of members of the House of Representatives following their appointment, and shall be reviewed again at the first general election of members of the House of Representatives after a lapse of ten (10) years, and in the same manner thereafter.

In cases mentioned in the foregoing paragraph, when the majority of the voters favors the dismissal of a judge, he shall be dismissed.

Matters pertaining to review shall be prescribed by law.

The judges of the Supreme Court shall be retired upon the attainment of the age as fixed by law.

All such judges shall receive, at regular stated intervals, adequate compensation which shall not be decreased during their terms of office.

Article 80. The judges of the inferior courts shall be appointed by the Cabinet from a list of persons nominated by the Supreme Court. All such judges shall hold office for a term of ten (10) years with privilege of reappointment, provided that they shall be retired upon the attainment of the age as fixed by law.

The judges of the inferior courts shall receive, at regular stated intervals, adequate compensation which shall not be decreased during their terms of office.

Article 81. The Supreme Court is the court of last resort with power to determine the constitutionality of any law, order, regulation or official act.

Article 82. Trials shall be conducted and judgment declared publicly.

Where a court unanimously determines publicity to be dangerous to public order or morals, a trial may be conducted privately, but trials of political offenses, offenses involving the press or cases wherein the rights of people as guaranteed in Chapter III of this Constitution are in question shall always be conducted publicly.

Chapter VII: Finance

Article 83. The power to administer national finances shall be exercised as the Diet shall determine.

Article 84. No new taxes shall be imposed or existing ones modified except by law or under such conditions as law may prescribe.

Article 85. No money shall be expended, nor shall the State obligate itself, except as authorized by the Diet.

Article 86. The Cabinet shall prepare and submit to the Diet for its consideration and decision a budget for each fiscal year.

Article 87. In order to provide for unforeseen deficiencies in the budget, a reserve fund may be authorized by the Diet to be expended upon the responsibility of the Cabinet.

The Cabinet must get subsequent approval of the Diet for all payments from the reserve fund.

Article 88. All property of the Imperial Household shall belong to the State. All expenses of the Imperial Household shall be appropriated by the Diet in the budget.

Article 89. No public money or other property shall be expended or appropriated for the use, benefit or maintenance of any religious institution or association, or for any charitable, educational or benevolent enterprises not under the control of public authority.

Article 90. Final accounts of the expenditures and revenues of the State shall be audited annually by a Board of Audit and submitted by the Cabinet to the Diet, together with the statement of audit, during the fiscal year immediately following the period covered.

The organization and competency of the Board of Audit shall be determined by law.

Article 91. At regular intervals and at least annually the Cabinet shall report to the Diet and the people on the state of national finances.

Chapter VIII: Local Self-Government

Article 92. Regulations concerning organization and operations of local public entities shall be fixed by law in accordance with the principle of local autonomy.

Article 93. The local public entities shall establish assemblies as their deliberative organs, in accordance with law.

The chief executive officers of all local public entities, the members of their assemblies, and such other local officials as may be determined by law shall be elected by direct popular vote within their several communities.

Article 94. Local public entities shall have the right to manage their property, affairs and administration and to enact their own regulations within law.

Article 95. A special law, applicable only to one local public entity, cannot be enacted by the Diet without the consent of the majority of the voters of the local public entity concerned, obtained in accordance with law.

Chapter IX: Amendments

Article 96. Amendments to this Constitution shall be initiated by the Diet, through a concurring vote of two-thirds or more of all the members of each House and shall thereupon be submitted to the people for ratification, which shall require the affirmative vote of a majority of all votes cast thereon, at a special referendum or at such election as the Diet shall specify.

Amendments when so ratified shall immediately be promulgated by the Emperor in the name of the people, as an integral part of this Constitution.

Chapter X: Supreme Law

Article 97. The fundamental human rights by this Constitution guaranteed to the people of Japan are fruits of the age-old struggle of man to be free; they have survived the many exacting tests for durability and are conferred upon this and future generations in trust, to be held for all time inviolate.

Article 98. This Constitution shall be the supreme law of the nation and no law, ordinance, imperial rescript or other act of government, or part thereof, contrary to the provisions hereof, shall have legal force or validity.

The treaties concluded by Japan and established laws of nations shall be faithfully observed.

Article 99. The Emperor or the Regent as well as Ministers of State, members of the Diet, judges, and all other public officials have the obligation to respect and uphold this Constitution.

Chapter XI: Supplementary Provisions

Article 100. This Constitution shall be enforced as from the day when the period of six months will have elapsed counting from the day of its promulgation.

The enactment of laws necessary for the enforcement of this Constitution, the election of members of the House of Councillors and the procedure for the convocation of the Diet and other preparatory procedures necessary for the enforcement of this Constitution may be executed before the day prescribed in the preceding paragraph.

Article 101. If the House of Councillors is not constituted before the effective date of this Constitution, the House of Representatives shall function as the Diet until such time as the House of Councillors shall be constituted.

Article 102. The term of office for half the members of the House of Councillors serving in the first term under this Constitution shall be three years. Members falling under this category shall be determined in accordance with law.

Article 103. The Ministers of State, members of the House of Representatives and judges in office on the effective date of this Constitution, and all other public officials who occupy positions corresponding to such positions as are recognized by this Constitution shall not forfeit their positions automatically on account of the enforcement of this Constitution unless otherwise specified by law. When, however, successors are elected or appointed under the provisions of this Constitution, they shall forfeit their positions as a matter of course.

INDEX

Y

About the Author

Tim Odagiri is an author and software architect with more than four decades of programming experience. Born Tim Patrick, his third-grade teacher introduced him to the riches of Japanese culture and language. He has authored a dozen books on subjects as diverse as technology, history, and humor. Tim earned his computer science degree from Seattle Pacific University. He currently lives in the Tokyo-metro area where he serves as director of the 日本＋YOU (Nihon Plus You) research center.

About the Series

In a world awash in nearly unlimited information, the *Understand in One Afternoon* series helps you discover the essentials of important subjects in a reasonable amount of time. Each book is designed to be consumed in about four hours—in one afternoon—and offers a core grounding on topics ranging from current events to technology, from philosophy to business.

Printed in Great Britain
by Amazon

30235873R00101